WorkLife Balance:
for all who struggle to juggle

(a WorkBook)

By Charlene Levis

WorkLife®

BALANCE + TAKE 5 + BACK 2 BASICS + JUST 4 FUN = 🏠

Follow me on Twitter @worklifecafe

WorkLife Balance: for all who struggle to juggle
Charlene Levis.
Self Improvement / Time Management / Work-Life
Non-fiction

ISBN: 978-0-9867904-0-9

Cover and interior design by Sandra Verhoeff, Signet Studio, www.signetstudio.com

Editor, Michael Blackstock, Kamloops, BC

Publisher website: www.worklifecafe.ca

Copies can be ordered on lulu.com or Amazon.com.

To my family, for their love and encouragement,
and for being fun

Acknowledgements

Thank you to my husband Michael and our sons for their ongoing support and encouragement. Michael, thank you, for insisting I publish this workbook, for maintaining our family balance while I wrote, and for taking on the role of VP of editing and publishing.

Thanks to the most wonderful parents and siblings anyone could ever wish for, and for teaching me the importance of "family first."

Thank you to Sandra Verhoeff of Signet Studio for believing in this project, taking my ideas and making them come to life through designs that consistently exceed expectations. You make everything I do look fantastic!

Thank you to my family, friends and associates who have endured my obsession with work-life topics for so many years. Jacqui for front-line insight into systems thinking and the day-to-day problems of those who struggle with the ultimate challenges, loss of loved ones, poor health and poverty; Bob for inspiration and advice; Patti for being my sounding board for ideas and enthusiastic supporter; Cathy, for enduring support and quality assurance; Noni for sparking and fueling my creativity; Jane for making sure I didn't forget the Fun; Vicki for living life with gusto; Tammy for being No. 1!; Susan and Mary for ideas and encouragement; Helen and Del for walking the work-life balance talk; Phyllis and Harvey for their encouragement, an open door and coffee breaks! Gailene for cherry strudel, fruit loops and insight about filling your soul; Shannon, Kathy, Deb, Linda and Liz for breaks from the day-to-day work-life juggle; Janice for helping plan my first work-life session years ago when there wasn't much interest in the topic of work-life balance; Harry, Cathy, Claire, and Michael for helping me become a better writer; Tina for being a life-long friend and giving this project a thumbs up; Dale for brainstorming; Willie for the next step idea and...My *Taking the Stage*® facilitator and colleagues who encouraged me to share this information.

Linda Duxbury, Canadian Researcher and work-life expert, whose work has been an influence since early in my career.

The topic of work-life balance is not new and I am convinced there are no new ideas. For example, Aristotle, Rousseau and other great philosophers were pondering and writing about work, life, and balance *way* 'back in the day', as have many subsequent writers. The writers who have been my most influential sources of information, ideas and inspiration are listed in the references and resources section.

Part of the success of an idea is finding the right moment.
I hope the work-life balance moment is now.

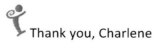
Thank you, Charlene

TABLE OF CONTENTS

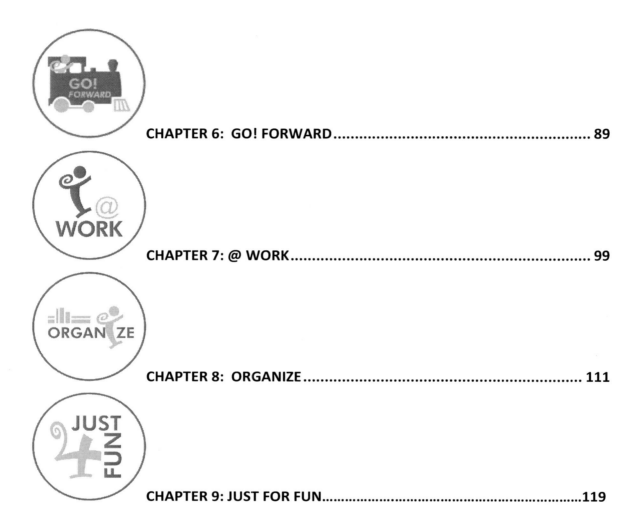

About this Book

Thank you for purchasing this book. I developed this *workbook* for people who are struggling with the work-life juggle. I hope that between these covers you will find some ideas and inspiration that may help you find a happier and healthier work-life balance.

Are you struggling to juggle all the demands on your time? Do you feel overwhelmed when you... look at your calendar; read the note from your child's school about an upcoming project; check your burgeoning email inbox; suddenly recall a missed birthday; get an overdue bill notice; or when your boss asks you to work extra hours or take on another high priority? How often do you have one of *those days* when things just don't go, at all, as planned? I'm thinking of when you get a call that your aging parent has had a fall, or your child is sick at school.

You are not alone. Studies illustrate that people all over the world are struggling to manage work-life responsibilities, and achieve a better balance. Our sense of balance is impacted by the forces and choices that influence our work and personal lives. Such as work and family responsibilities, unexpected events and challenges, luring opportunities, impending deadlines, extra curricular activities and interests.

These influencing forces and choices can put us out of balance. We know we should be taking better care ~ exercising regularly, eating healthy food, getting enough sleep, and spending time with family and friends. But, when we don't have enough time and are struggling to juggle, we start compromising and coping in unhealthy ways.

Additionally, the current economic climate and financial worries add to our stress. The cost of living is rising, salaries and wages are not. It's getting harder to make ends meet. The security of our jobs and retirement may be in question. In this case, a fundamental premise of our wellbeing is threatened: financial security. If we still have a job, we feel lucky. If we are overwhelmed or over-worked we may be hesitant to raise these concerns with our employer in fear that this could put our job in jeopardy.

Of course, managing work and family responsibilities would be easier if the system was working with us, instead of against us. The world of work has changed. There are more dual income families, technology blurs the line between work and personal time, the workforce is aging and today's workers have different expectations of work. Unfortunately, changes in public and workplace policy and practices are long overdue. Most workers know this. Progressive thinkers like Carol Evans of *Working Mother Magazine* in the United States, Dr. Linda Duxbury in Canada, and Dr. Clare Kelliher in the UK, have been working to draw attention to this issue for years. Government and employers are now recognizing the mounting social and corporate costs of stress-related illness resulting from our struggle to juggle. Change is on the horizon. In the meantime, we need to help ourselves find a happier and healthier balance between work and life. *And that's what this book is about.*

This book represents my effort to help people improve their work-life balance and to contribute to the discussion on this important topic. I also have a loftier goal, as I believe that there are synergies between work-life balance and sustainability. The way we are currently living is not sustainable on any level. Living more simply, and in balance, is better on a personal level, as well as for the health and sustainability of our families, our communities, our workplaces, and our planet. It's time for change.

Where should we start, big or small? E.F. Schumacher, in his book *Small is Beautiful: Economics as if People Mattered* (1973), advised us to study *"the possibilities of alternative methods of production and patterns of living — so as to get off the collision course on which we are moving with ever-increasing speed"*. We are all part of one big complex system. Small changes towards living a healthier and balanced life can make a big difference by inspiring a philosophical shift towards taking better care of ourselves, our families and our planet. Let's face it, when we're exhausted and overwhelmed, all we can manage sometimes is one small thing. But that's ok, because even seemingly small changes can make a big difference. For example, by adjusting your work hours, occasionally working from home, or zigging while others zag, you can have a positive influence on transportation systems and commuting patterns. This approach may reduce the amount of driving we do, and maybe even help reduce carbon emissions. More importantly, you could be home more often to share a family meal... *and that's worth thinking about.*

I started my company, WorkLife Innovations, in 1998, and my mission statement: *to promote work-life innovations that sustain people, productivity and the planet,* is inspired by Schumacher's *small is beautiful* principles.

Defining work-life balance is complicated. Spending 50% of our time on "work" and 50% on "life" DOES NOT EQUAL balance. Balance is a sense of harmony and contentment that waxes and wanes over weeks, seasons of the year, or even a lifetime. It comes from being able to weave your way through your day without an undue amount of stress and pressure.

For some of us, being out of balance is a factor of choice, that is an unintended consequence of over-filling our plate at the smorgasbord of life. An overflowing plate means more things in the air, more to juggle, and thus more struggle. In this case, advice like reducing extra-curricular activities or turning off your blackberry may be helpful. For others, being out of balance is a result of circumstance or challenges such as serious health or family issues, poverty or being a single parent.

I realize there is no one-size-fits-all solution to balance, and that you may have chosen this book because you are tired-out by life's hectic pace. That's why this book is designed as an easy to use work-life-friendly workbook, so that you can define and refine what balance looks like for you, in a way that works for you. Now, let's take a look at how the book is organized.

WorkLife Balance: for all who struggle to juggle, begins with a balance check in Chapter One, where you can assess your state of balance. In Chapter Two, we spend some time touring the work-life landscape, as this provides the context for the key part of the book which is building your own work-life plan and work-life framework for decision-making. The remaining chapters provide information, ideas and tools to help you achieve a happier and healthier balance between work and life.

The basic premise of this book is **TAKE 5**, which reflects an idea that small changes can make a big difference. Take 5 encourages you to; become mindful of activities that promote a sense of balance and wellbeing, find magic in special moments that life offers, and make it a habit to incorporate short healthy breaks and balancing activities in your daily routine. Another premise is **BACK 2 BASICS** that reflects simplicity, and encourages the old-fashioned-way, using pencil or pen and paper as thinking and planning tools, for example.

Information is conveyed by using textual, interactive and inspirational visual images. The images are designed to be cues and clues, and then become reminders. So, if the words don't stick with you, maybe an image or exercise will. I've organized the workbook in chapters that include a collection of exercises and ideas that may help with a particular work-life challenge. It's not necessary to read from cover to cover. Please browse, flip pages, shuffle, and skim until you see a page that resonates with you; a page that makes sense for you in that moment. I do encourage you, however, to read and complete the exercises in Chapter Two, which is about creating your personal work-life balance plan and work-life framework. In my view, this completed framework is a key success factor in moving towards a happier and healthier balance.

I am no poster Mom for work-life balance. I've figured out a few things, but I'm struggling to juggle too. I'll always regret postponing tucking in my oldest son when he was little. I'd be at my computer *getting one last thing done* when he'd call me to come and say good-night. *"I'll be there in a minute",* I'd say. By the time I went to tuck him in he was often asleep. Tucking him in would only have taken a few minutes and I wish I would have made a different choice. *Remember you can't get time back!*

Keep this book handy, and when you're struggling with a work-life challenge, flip through, and hopefully you will find something helpful. This book is *your* WorkLife Balance Workbook. So, go ahead, write in it, make it yours, discuss your concerns and ideas with family and friends, and make up a great plan for your work-life balance!

Charlene

> *I need calm and quiet if I am to work, but I need a certain amount of stimulation, too.*
> *It's really a juggling act. I must be a gatekeeper on the traffic in my life.*
> *Too much traffic and I grow overwhelmed. Too little and I grow stagnant.*
> *It's a balance that I am seeking and I must be attentive*
> *because my needs are always shifting.*
>
> Julia Cameron, Author of *The Artist's Way Trilogy.*
> *Finding Water, The Art of Perseverance.*
> 2009. Pg., 241.

1

Chapter 1:
BALANCE CHECK

I'm guessing you may have purchased this book because you feel like you are out of balance and struggling to juggle? Most of us know when we are out of balance. We know whether we should be... exercising more, getting more sleep, rushing less, attending to important things, having more fun, and feeling less stress!

But, sometimes our lives are *so busy* we don't even have time to stop and reflect about how things are going. So, let's jump right in and start with a balance check. The first exercise here is called (un) balancing forces. When you want to do a quick check-in to see how you are doing, you can use this one page exercise.

Remember, work-life balance is not a formula like: spending 50% of your time on "work" and 50% of your time on "life" = balance. Nor is work only paid work. Some of the most important work in our society is not paid work ~ like childcare, eldercare, housework and volunteer work! It's complicated. Balance is more of a feeling or way of being, and an important one of multiple factors contributing to a state of overall wellbeing. *Life is better with balance.*

These exercises are designed to help you reflect on your current work-life balance. Choose the one that will work best for you, and re-visit when things in your life change, or you're feeling overwhelmed. If you are feeling overwhelmed, this chapter also includes a suggestion for getting *back to basics.*

BALANCE CHECK ~ (UN) BALANCING FORCES

This is not a quiz. This exercise is designed to help you reflect on some of the factors, or in this case forces, that are pushing you out of balance, or could potentially pull you back into balance. You can use this page as a quick balance check or spend a bit more time thinking about your check-in by considering the questions on the next page.[1]

Step 1: Check all that apply.

Unbalancing or Pushing Force		Balancing or Pull force
O In a rut or depressed[2]		O A sense of purpose
O Not enough sleep		O Enough sleep
O Not enough exercise		O Enough exercise
O Too much or NO work		O Work in control
O Worried about money		O Financially secure
O Errands undone		O Errands done
O Family worries	**BALANCE** ▲	O Family doing well
O Aging parents		O Aging parents plan
O No time for friends		O Time with friends
O Unhealthy eating		O Healthy eating
O Not enough Fun ☹		O Enough fun ☺
O Noisy life		O Quiet moments
O Being Late		O Being on time
O Missing deadlines		O Meeting deadlines
O No real support network		O Support network

[1] Find additional copies of this Balance Check Worksheet in Chapter 8 and at the WorkLife Café website. For more information about downloading **FREE** copies of this exercise and other colourful workbook resources, see Chapter 8.

[2] It's critical to seek help when overwhelmed or depressed!

Step 2: You are not alone!

The purpose of this exercise is to encourage awareness. If this leaves you feeling like you are out of balance, *remember you are not alone!* Research shows that work-life conflict is a common and serious concern in countries across the globe, and most of us compensate by not getting enough sleep, not exercising, eating poorly, compromising on family time, chores and work. More on this later on. *In the meantime...*

Step 3: Think about the following.

> *"Problems arise in that one has to find a balance between*
> *what people need from you and*
> *what you need for yourself."*
> Jessye Norman, American Opera Singer.

What's Working? ☺

What do you need for yourself? Your main concerns.

Step 4: Make a plan. (Need ideas? This book should help).

What ideas do you have for getting your needs met and restoring balance, or seeking support?

BALANCE CHECK ~ WHAT'S ON YOUR PLATE?

What's on your Plate? is an adaptation of 'the wheel of life' or the pie exercise. This popular exercise will help you consider the 'big picture'.

Step 1: What's on your plate?

In each section of the diagram, on the following page, write down one key word for each responsibility, focus or interest area in your life. These are unique and personal, but consider; family and friends, home, personal health and development, learning, finances, hobbies, career, community, environment, giving back, fun, spiritual, or others.

Then picture what success in each area means to you, and write a few clarifying thoughts.

Note: This exercise may be easier once you've completed the exercises in Chapter Two.

Step 2: Take 1

Sit quietly and look at what's on your plate. *What do you see and feel? Are you dedicating your time, energy, money to the most important areas of your life?*

Step 3: Take 2

In many cultures there is a four-fold view that includes **physical, intellectual, emotional and spiritual** (mind, body and spirit) wellbeing and needs. Now, look again at what's on your plate, and check that each of these needs is being met.

Step 4: Do I need to adjust?

If you want to make some adjustments ask yourself:

What would I need to do more of, or less of, to achieve a healthier balance?

What would I need to do more of, or less of, to achieve my goals?

Are my goals realistic given my current responsibilities? If not, consider taking some items off your list or putting them on the backburner for now.

Can I do things differently? Think of one thing, that is do-able and would make a positive difference. For example, combine a goal to get fit and spend more time with friends by walking with a friend.

Don't be afraid to say: *"Sorry, I've got too much on my plate right now".*

> *A NO uttered from the deepest conviction*
> *is better than a yes merely uttered to please,*
> *or what is worse, to avoid trouble.*
>
> Mahatma Gandhi

BALANCE CHECK ~ WHAT'S ON YOUR PLATE?

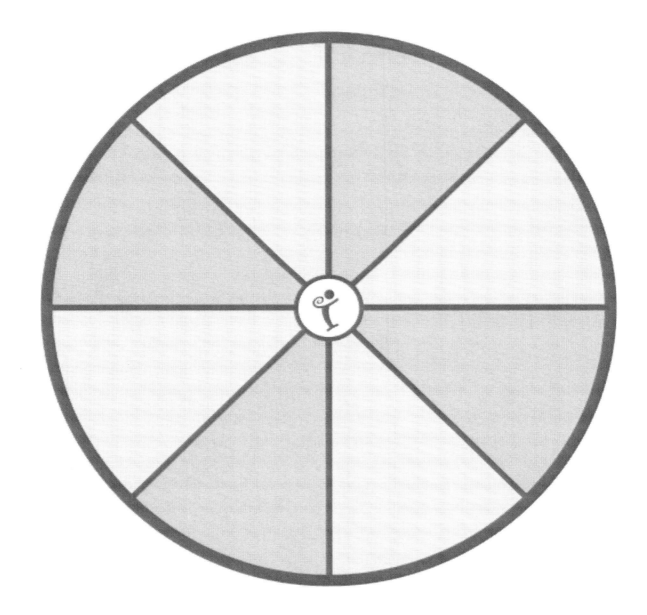

Date: _____

- Completing the exercises in Chapter 2, Your WorkLife Framework, is a key success factor in helping to maintain balance. There are other exercises in this workbook that I hope are helpful. *However, …*

- **…if you are overwhelmed:** Ask for help from family, friends or professionals.

- Take the WorkLife Balance Quiz, and Stress Assessment, at Canadian Mental Health Association http://www.cmha.ca and review the information on these important topics, including when and where to get help.

- Watch Randy Pausch, Ph.D. ~ The Last Lecture, and Time Management Lecture (long and sad, but provocative ~ 60+ mins.) http://download.srv.cs.cmu.edu/~pausch/

- **Great News! A FREE ONE-YEAR MEMBERSHIP TO THE WORKLIFE CAFÉ** is included with your purchase of this workbook, and entitles you to download Workbook Resources. Visit the WorkLife Café at http://www.worklifecafe.ca . Follow the link for FREE Resources. Type in the username: worklifecafe   password: take5 ~ all lower case.

I'VE GOT TOO MUCH ON MY PLATE!

"I've got too much on my plate right now!"[3] When a crisis strikes, you feel overwhelmed, or you're having a meltdown because you can't keep up, it's time to get *back to basics*. Decide what stays on your plate and what has to come off. Think of this like being lost in the woods. You retreat to the basics of staying safe and warm. You call for help. You take all the non-essential items off your list. You let go of unrealistic expectations.

Step 1: Assess your situation.

Consider the big picture. You can use the Mind Map on the next page to jot down some thoughts about the following: *What are you dealing with right now? How are you managing day-to-day? How are you coping?*

Try not to compare yourself to others.

Step 2: Identify your basics.

Are the basics such as your personal health, family and finances attended to? What are the key things that need your attention at this time? What kind of attention is needed? The balance checks in this chapter can help you identify if you've got too much on your plate.

Step 3: Make some choices.

Now, decide what stays on your plate and what has to come off, at least in the short term. Identify systems, routines or assistance you need to help you stay organized, save time, reduce your stress or cope. Ask for help when you need it!

Step 4: What's your plan? (Need ideas? see the tips on the left.)

---

[3] (See the previous exercise *"What's on Your Plate?"*)

Brainstorming Session
M**I**NDMAP

Name _____

Date _____

Remember to post in a visible spot!

PLEASE RECYCLE

References & Resources
- Mind Mapping idea from Tony Buzan
- Check out this link for more mind map inspiration
  www.mindmapinspiration.com

2

Chapter 2:

WORKLIFE BALANCE FRAMEWORK

Like most things in life, to be successful you have to have a vision, goal, plan and strategies. This chapter provides an overview of the WorkLife Landscape, and includes exercises and ideas to help clarify your goals and plans and to create a WorkLife Framework.

A WorkLife Framework is a valuable tool for making decisions and choices, maintaining work-life balance, and achieving goals. When we make poor choices it can compromise what is really important. And, because "balance" will look different at different age and life stages, this chapter also includes tools for defining and refining balance.

While all other sections of this book are designed to be used as and when required, this one is essential. *Why?* Because y*our WorkLife Framework is a key success factor to achieving and maintaining balance.* So, let's get started!

THE WORKLIFE LANDSCAPE

The topic of work-life balance is so important because the time crunch and resulting work-life tension impacts our ability to attend to our basic needs. When we don't have adequate resources, like the time to meet our work and family commitments, we start compromising on sleep, diet, and time with family and friends. Our sense of wellbeing and balance is thrown off.

The following interpretation of Abraham Maslow's Hierarchy of Needs, published in his 1943 paper: *A Theory of Human Motivation*, helps us see the connection between work-life balance and basic human needs.

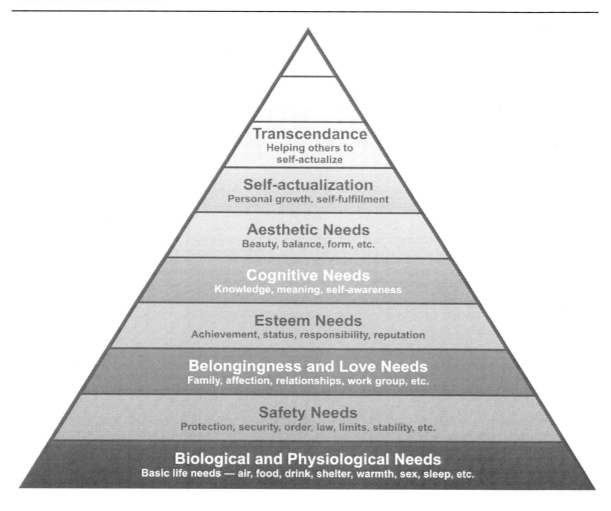

MASLOW'S HIERARCHY OF NEEDS

What's the link between Maslow's Hierarchy of Needs and Work-Life Balance?

Research has identified some of the key contributors to wellbeing and longevity. A few common themes are emerging: [4]

- Have purpose
- Don't Smoke
- Put family first
- Be active everyday
- Keep socially engaged
- Eat a healthy diet including fruits, vegetables and whole grains
- Get enough sleep
- Drink enough water
- Drink red wine (in moderation), and eat some dark chocolate. ☺

BUT, how can we …

- put family first, for example by sharing a family meal;
- be active everyday;
- eat a healthy diet;
- keep socially engaged;
- and get enough sleep!

...if we don't have enough time?

And, we don't have enough time, in Canada anyway. According to Roy Romanov, Chair of the Canadian Centre for Wellbeing commenting on findings from *Caught in the Time Crunch* (2010):

"People are struggling to meet the competing demands of a workplace that can reach out to them 24/7, caring for children and aging parents, and their own need to refresh body and mind. As individuals and as a society we are paying a steep price for this time crunch. We're less healthy, both physically and mentally and we have less time for leisure and relaxation with family."

---

[4]Buettner, Dan. *National Geographic*. The Secrets of Living Longer. November 2005, reporting on a study of places that produce a high number of centenarians and better than average health. Having good genes also helps! http://ngm.nationalgeographic.com/ngm/0511/feature1/index.html

---

THE WORKLIFE LANDSCAPE

Canadian researchers and work-life experts, Linda Duxbury and Chris Higgins, found that Canadians have 'role-overload' and 'interference' between work and family. Canadians tend to cope with this work-life conflict through strategies like cutting back on personal time, family time, housework, social life, sleep and even having children. They work harder or compromise on quality of work, and some take prescription medicine or drink. These strategies *"benefit no one: employees, their families, employers or Canadian society in general."*[5]

Ipso Reid surveys show that 'the level of stress in modern Canadian society is spilling out a lot of negatives.' Darrell Bricker and John Wright of Ipso Reid reported the following about Canadian workers in *What Canadians Think: about almost everything.* (2006)

- 74% feel they have less free time now than they did five years ago.
- 55% reported physical and mental stress in the workplace.
- 42% would like to work from home at least one day a week.
- 69% come in early or leave late to keep up with their workload.
- 59% say they often skip lunch or eat at their desk in order to leave work on time.
- 40% feel out of control!

Canadians are not alone. Throughout the world work-life issues are now recognized as one of the top factors contributing to stress-related illness, workplace absenteeism, presenteeism (at work but going through the motions due to ill health and/or worry) and having a serious impact on productivity and corporate profitability.[6] It's pretty obvious if employees are struggling the employer incurs both direct and indirect costs.

In addition, adding to our worry and stress are financial troubles, intensified by economic downturns, that reduce our ability to buy services and products that might help us maintain balance ~ such as home maintenance services, help with family responsibilities, or the occasional dinner out.

The topic of work-life balance is newsworthy! Canada's esteemed newspaper the *Globe and Mail* featured a weeklong discussion about the work-life balance crisis in Canada, in the series 'Canada: Our Time to Lead.' The lead in to the front-page feature, 'Stress: How Your Busy Life Is Killing You' was *"Work-life balance is not just a personal challenge - it's a looming public health crisis."* The article described how *'chronic stress hurts body and mind and is costing health-care and corporate Canada billions every year.'* (October 30, pg: 1, A12-A13.)

---

[5] Duxbury, Linda and Higgins, Chris. 2008. *Reducing Work-Life Conflict; What works? What doesn't?*

[6] Buck Consultants. 2009. *Global Wellness Survey* of 1,103 organizations representing more than 45 countries and 10 million employees.

The following quotes are from the *Globe and Mail:* 'Stress: How Your Busy Life Is Killing You.'[7]

"Chronic stress caused by taking on too much – both at home and at work – has been linked to a wide range of serious health concerns, from Alzheimer's and depression to obesity, diabetes and heart disease."

"The physical and psychological ailments brought about by stress are believed to be a major reason absentee rates for full-time employees have shot up 21 per cent in the past 10 years. At least one think tank estimates that stress-related absences cost [Canadian] employers more than $10-billion a year, with an additional $14-billion impact on the health-care system."

Harvard researcher Lisa Berman recently studied the impact different types of supervisors can have: *"The stunning thing we found was that managers who scored very low on creativity in managing work-family conflicts had employees who scored much higher in terms of their cardiovascular risk…. They were more likely to have diabetes, they were more likely to have hypertension, they were more likely to be over-weight, than people with managers who were more adaptive."*

When it comes to managing work-family conflict, the essentials, it seems, are a supportive manager and a supportive workplace culture that allow for some flexibility in work arrangements, or at least the perception of flexibility, which is what Duxbury and Higgins found was important. This conclusion is supported by research showing that people do better at work when they have a sense of control over their time and how their work gets done. Giving people a bit more control over their time and work is essential to managing the work-life juggle.

There is mounting evidence that strategies and initiatives that support work-life balance significantly improve employee wellbeing, reduce absenteeism and turnover, and improve workforce engagement, productivity and corporate profitability.

A global push for change in workplace culture is occurring.

Governments and employers now realize it's in their best interest to pay attention to work-life balance and the need for workplace flexibility, to mitigate the increasing and pervasive costs of stress-related illness.

The White House Forum on Workplace Flexibility held on March 31, 2010, drew worldwide attention to this issue and inspired a cascade of initiatives and increased commitment to address work-life balance and bring about positive structural change in the world of work. *"President Obama wrapped up the day's program with remarks reinforcing his administration's*

---

[7] *Globe and Mail*, 2010. 'Stress: How your busy life is killing you.' October 30, pg 1, A12-13.

commitment to this issue ~ not just as a "women's issue," but as an issue that affects the wellbeing of our families, the success of our businesses, and the future of our nation's economy."

The Corporate Executive Board reported findings from a survey of 50,000 employees indicating work–life balance ranks as one of the most important workplace attributes ~ second only to compensation ~ and employees who feel they have a better work–life balance tend to work 21% harder than those that don't. [8]

In Canada, and many other countries, the legislative framework provides some support for work-life balance, such as through human rights laws which prohibit discriminatory practices in employment based on criteria including gender, ability, family status and other grounds. Both the UK and Australia have introduced 'Right 2 Request' [flexible work arrangements] legislation, which obligates employers to at least review and consider requests for flexible work arrangements. Implementing flexible work arrangements has its share of challenges. However, I'm hopeful about the potential more workplace flexibility offers.

In my view, we need a little wiggle-room at work to effectively manage our work and personal responsibilities. A little room to take a healthy break, a little room to attend to a family or personal commitment or unexpected event, and a little respect for our basic need to succeed in both work and life.

At **WorkLife®** we believe a bit of flexibility and respect goes a long ways towards improving personal and work results. And that is reflected in the tag line of my human resources consulting firm, WorkLife HR Solutions: **Flexibility. Respect. Results.** We promote flexible work arrangements ~ FLEX! ~ as an opportunity to inspire positive change in the workplace and beyond. We believe in changing the way people work and live, *when the traditional way no longer makes sense.* And we hope that you do too!

John Stackhouse, Editor-In-Chief, *The Globe and Mail* introduced the 'Our Time to Lead' discussions, including the discussion about Canada's work-life balance crisis, referenced here earlier, with these powerful words:

> "We hope, and intend, for this discussion to strike at the heart of how Canadians define ourselves, and our nation. It is meant to go beyond words. We hope it will become a turning point.
>
> We need to re-examine Canadian institutions, and conceits, that we hold dear. Instead of locking ourselves in celebrations of the past, we want to explore our future — and all we can do to make it brilliant... We hope these discussions ignite a million great Canadian debates, at breakfast tables and board tables..."

---

[8] Corporate Executive Board. 2009. http://www.executiveboard.com/businessweek/bw-week9.html

Remember, you are not alone and continue the conversation!

Just bring up the topic of work-life balance among friends and work colleagues that you trust and you might be surprised at how many people are feeling the same way. Talking about these topics is a great way to share ideas and come up with solutions.

I hope this book provides some information, ideas and inspiration to help you achieve a happier and healthier work-life balance, and that it will also make a positive contribution to this important conversation.

Now,

let's get started building your WorkLife Framework ~

CONFIRM YOUR NEEDS, VALUES AND PURPOSE

Developing a work-life plan starts with reflecting on what's important to you as well as clarifying your big idea, goals or dream.

Step 1: Values check.

Think about your most important needs, values and priorities. In the table below, check off all that seem relevant or add more in the blank spaces.

Values Check		
○ Hard Working	○ Spending time with family	○ Having Fun
○ Financially Secure	○ Making a Difference	○ Being Honest
○ Helping Others	○ Making a Contribution	○ Being Positive
○ Being Friendly	○ Being Knowledgeable	○ Being Reliable
○ Being a Leader	○ Caring for the Environment	○ Being Happy
○ Being Healthy	○ Encouraging and Supporting others	○ Work-Life Balance
○ Healthy Living	○ Spending time with friends	○ Being Adventurous
○ Always Learning	○ Having Flexibility	○ Being Wealthy
○ Being Funny	○ Being a great mother, father, sister, brother, friend, community leader, friend, volunteer or _____	
○ Sharing Knowledge	○	○
○	○	○
○	○	○

Now, look over your list and circle or highlight those that are **most important** to you.

Step 2: Clarify your life purpose, your big idea or dream.

Sit quietly and picture your ideal life ~ or even a day will work. Consider these questions: *What would you be doing? What do you want to; be, do, accomplish, contribute, experience or have in your life? What is your purpose? What values are most important to you? What are your greatest strengths and skills? What do you most enjoy?* You can use the Mind Map provided for flushing out ideas.

Describe your purpose, your big idea or dream here.

- It can be helpful to dig deeper using the question: *why?* Keep asking why until you settle on the answer. If one of your goals is to have more money ask: *WHY do I want more money? How will that make me feel?* If the answer is more secure then the actual goal may be financial security. In this case, the goal or focus changes to *I want to be financially secure.*

- Remember plans can change as priorities and resources shift. So when things in your work-life change you might want to revisit these exercises.

Brainstorming Session
M**I**NDMAP

Name _____

Date _____

Remember to post in a visible spot!

PLEASE RECYCLE

References & Resources
- Mind Mapping idea from Tony Buzan
- Check out this link for more mind map inspiration
  www.mindmapinspiration.com

Step 3: Write down your ideas for achieving your dream.

Step 4: Write down the key goals and next action/steps.

As you probably know, **a good goal is SMART**: Specific, Measureable, Achievable, Rewarded, and Time-bound.

Goal:
Next Actions/Steps:
O
O
O
O
Goal:
Next Actions/Steps:
O
O
O
O

Keep these goals in mind during the next step of developing your WorkLife Timeline and WorkLife Framework.

CREATE A WORKLIFE TIMELINE

Developing a timeline helps you clarify your work-life priorities and goals, make better choices, and keep your life in balance.

A work-life timeline, like the sample below, is a helpful long-range planning tool that provides an overview of work-life priorities at different age and life stages. For example, a young adult may be focused on education, job and spending time with friends. Later life may become much more complicated by adding a career and young family. Work-life during this young family stage may be characterized by just struggling to get enough sleep, and make it through the next day! Finding balance at this stage can be incredibly difficult. Having a plan is key.

A timeline gives you a heads-up for planning and scheduling by highlighting important information like children becoming independent and leaving home, underscoring the need for optimizing family time during their younger years.

SAMPLE:

Next 5–10 years: 2011-2016		
My Age	Milestones & Key Dates	WorkLife Priorities and Goals
50-55	Kids graduate high school Kids driving Kids working	Family Time Planning for Retirement Planning for University Flexible Work Hours Kids Athletics and School Commitments

Next year:		
My Age	Milestones & Key Dates	WorkLife Priorities and Goals
50	50th Birthdays!	Family Time (Milestone Birthdays)! Finances Fun Healthy Living/Balance

Seasons: This provides an overview of upcoming events and regular tasks. [9]

Winter	Spring	Summer	Fall
Ski & Hibernate	Spring Cleaning Lacrosse	Big Birthdays Family Vacation	Winterize Back to School

---

[9] This idea is adapted from *Simplify your Time* by Marcia Ramsland. I recommend this book!

MY WORKLIFE TIMELINE

Next 5-10 years: _____

My Age	Milestones and Key Dates (for me and others close to me).	WorkLife Priorities and Goals

Current year: _____

My Age	Milestones and Key Dates (for me and others close to me).	WorkLife Priorities and Goals

Seasons of the current year: _____

MY WORKLIFE TIMELINE ~ Long Range ~ by Season

Seasons of year: _____

Winter	Spring	Summer	Fall

Seasons of year: _____

Winter	Spring	Summer	Fall

Seasons of year: _____

Winter	Spring	Summer	Fall

BUILD YOUR WORKLIFE FRAMEWORK

A WorkLife Framework can help you clarify both your work and life goals, make better choices, and keep your life in balance. You can use this exercise to create a framework for your work, personal/family life or both.

Use your answers to the following questions to complete the WorkLife Framework exercise on the page after next. If deciding on a family framework, include your family in the planning process described below.

Step 1: Choose key words to summarize your work-life purpose, priorities and goals.

The previous exercises helped clarify your current values, needs, goals, priorities and responsibilities. Think about these exercises and **find one key word** to characterize each priority area or goal. *Narrow this down to your top 3 current priorities.*

Step 2: Clarify what the key word means.

Think about the key word and what behaviours and/or habits would demonstrate a commitment to that priority.

Step 3: Identify a role model as a benchmark or barometer for your framework.

Sometimes it can help to have role model who has succeeded at something you're trying to attain. When my husband and I are thinking we need to have more "fun" we think about what our friends Shannon and James would do.

Step 4: Use your WorkLife Framework to check and adjust.

Use your WorkLife Framework to help you think about whether goals and plans are "do-able" given your current work-life priorities. Or, when you have a decision to make such as whether to attend an event, make a purchase, or change your job, check it against your WorkLife Framework. Using this framework helps maintain a healthy and balanced work-lifestyle.

Ask yourself: *Am I spending my time, money and energy on the areas of my work and /or life that are most important (consistent with my values)? How will this decision impact my current priorities? For example: how will this decision impact: my family, my finances, my fun and my overall ability to sustain a healthy work-life balance?*

Reminder: always consider resources such as budget, health and safety, time, energy, support systems, and other relevant concerns. Also, remember to re-evaluate your framework from time to time, as your work-life priorities change.

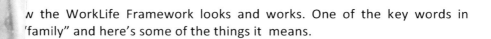

...w the WorkLife Framework looks and works. One of the key words in ...'family" and here's some of the things it means.

...t does this look like and what does it mean?	Role Model?
Family is first.	Mom and Dad
We pick our kids up from school, on time!	
We honour family commitments.	
We prepare, and share a healthy family meal.	
We have family nights, family holidays.	
We celebrate family events.	
Etc.	

...n to make I think about my key word, in this case "family."

...eting at 3:00 pm I think ~ **how will that impact my family?**

... is at 3:00 pm and I've committed to being on time for school pick-up. ...unless the meeting is really important or related to some other important ...ht also consider: *how will this impact my finances?* As finances is another ...ork.

BUILD YOUR WORKLIFE FRAMEWORK

Key Word	What does this look like, and what does it mean?	Role Model?

WRITE THE THREE KEY WORDS IN YOUR WORKLIFE FRAMEWORK HERE:	

3

Chapter 3:
BACK TO BASICS

Having basics in place, including strategies, systems and routines for managing, makes it easier to manage the work-life juggle. This chapter provides some suggestions and ideas for establishing the basics and dealing with common work-life challenges like; time management, information overload, decision-making, and planning.

MAKE TIME YOUR FRIEND

There is so much pressure to get things done. Being on the *treadmill of getting things done* can be stressful and overwhelming. A common lament seems to be *"there's not enough time"*. To make matters worse, there's a growing body of research telling us a once recommended strategy, multi-tasking to get things done, is out! *So what's in?* Change your relationship with time. Make time your friend!

Step 1: Assess your relationship with time.

Consider the big picture. *Do you feel like you have enough time? If not, what are the main things that you find are left undone or the reasons that you think there's not enough time? Are you often late or rushing? What are your time and energy zappers?* You might already know the answers to these questions or you may need to mull this over for a few days.

Step 2: Identify your top time wasters, energy zappers and solutions.

Write down your top 3 time wasters here. Then read over the ideas on the next few pages to see if there are some ideas you can use as possible solutions. Pay attention to what works and what doesn't work. Do more of what works!

Challenges:	Solutions:

MAKE TIME YOUR FRIEND

Check or underline any of the following tips you think might be helpful.

Use a daily planner and a calendar system.

○ **Find a planning system and calendar that works for you.** Then use it!

○ **Use Your WorkLife Framework to Keep the Big Picture, Goal or Dream in mind.** Know your top priorities. This helps you decide what goes in your calendar.

○ **Say NO!** Make it a habit to ask: *Is this the best use of my time right now given my current goals and priorities?* Don't hesitate to say *"No" or "Sorry, I've got too much on my plate right now"* when activities are not in line with your current priorities or when you are over-committed. To effectively manage the work-life juggle trade-offs are often required.

○ **Next action/steps are key to accomplishing goals.** Take your big goal and break it into **small action steps**, then identify the **next action.**   **Action/steps** start with action: call, research, shop for, write, edit, tidy, plan…

○ A **5 year plan**. This plan is intended as a *quick* overview of coming milestone events like a graduation, birthday or anniversary. Note these dates in your calendar system.

○ A **1 year plan.** This plan gives you an instant overview and heads up to ensure key events and dates for the coming year are scheduled and noted in your calendar, like an annual vacation. I like the quarterly or seasonal view.

○ A **1-month-ahead plan**. Get in the habit of completing your calendar for a minimum of the next 30 days. This helps prevent overloading your schedule and missing out on important dates. Keeping a 1-month calendar posted in a visible spot is key.

○ **A weekly plan and routines**. My favourite calendar view is week-by-week. It's easy to see when things are getting too frantic and this view corresponds with the natural rhythm of society. It can also be helpful to schedule weekly routines. For example: in our house Tuesday is work like heck Tuesday before my WorkLife Wednesday which is usually deadline day; Friday morning is usually for tidy up and errands, updating calendars and planning; Friday night is family night; weekends are usually sports or away days.

○ **Use a Weekly Menu Planner.** Using a menu planner makes a big difference. It's a time saver, a money saver and reduces stress. It can also help make meal planning and preparation more of a family affair. Simplify meal planning by including one-pot meals and slow cooker dishes, and making some meals predictable, like Friday, Pizza night. You can find a weekly menu planner and shopping list in Chapter 8, and a full colour version on the WorkLife Café website.

○ **Use a Weekly Review System.** A weekly review is recommended by David Allen of *Getting Things Done*. Really worth checking out if your work-life is busy, and even if it's not. Check here: http://tinyurl.com/2fufmzn. Also, remember to think about balance.

○ **Distinguish between events that are negotiable and non-negotiable**, and have a system for recording these. I still prefer a paper planner, so tentative and negotiable items are entered in pencil, non-negotiable, like a family birthday or a project deadline in pen. When things get too busy the tentative and negotiable items need to go!

The basics:

○ **Have a daily plan and get in the habit of having an evening review**. Have a daily plan that you review the evening before. Refine your plan for the next day, it helps you get a head start, be prepared and minimizes surprises.

○ **Simplify.** Ok, I admit to stealing this tip from the Quaker Oats Instant Oatmeal pack. Establish routines that make your day easier. Routines like: spending a few minutes at night ensuring you're ready for the next day and unloading the dishwasher; knowing that Saturday is pancake day; and the 1st of the month is change the furnace filter day.

○ **Re-think and Reduce.** Too often we feel pressure to accumulate more and more life experiences and stuff. When we get more stuff we need more stuff, when we do more life is busier. Think twice about getting more, and doing more.

○ **Prioritize:** Make it a habit to think: *if I could only get 1 thing on my "to do" list done today what would that be?* Get that done and then if your day goes sideways at least 1 thing is done. **Remember the 80/20 Rule.** The Pareto Principle says 20% of activities produce 80% of results. Accomplishing 1 important thing everyday for a year = 365 accomplishments! 1 a week = 52 ! **Think about that!**

○ **Group similar activities.** For example, group errands that requiring running around like grocery shopping; or group tasks that require computer work, like responding to email. If you're continually running out to the store for forgotten items, or responding to email and text messages there's a good chance you're wasting time. Think about it.

○ **Use the two minute rule.** If something you need to do will take two minutes or less, get it done. Time management expert David Allen recommends this strategy.

○ **NO Rabbit Holes (distractions).** I'm a researcher and can easily get distracted with some new topic to research. To keep me focused my husband put a sign by my computer that says "No Rabbit Holes". You could always post your work-life framework, your key goals or pictures to remind you of your priorities.

○ **Manage Your Email/Texting/Social Media, don't let it manage you!!** Unless it's required for your job, or you are worried about an emergency ~ only check/send messages a few

---

times a day. (**Always** *have a back up plan for emergency contact* when you rely on electronics such as cell phones, just in case the phone is lost or stops working!) Send meaningful messages with relevant subject lines. Be respectful of peoples' private time and consider whether messaging is the best choice for getting the job done. Maybe old-fashioned phoning would work. Be a good role model and perhaps the people messaging you will also learn better habits. (David Allen and Julia Morgenstern have great work-life and e-mail management strategies. One of Julia's tips is the name of her book: *Never Check E-mail in the Morning.*)

○ **Invest time up front.** I learned this from my husband who would spend a few minutes creating something out of a cardboard box that our kids would then play in for hours. The same goes for making critical home maintenance tasks a priority, putting systems in place like storage, filing or bookkeeping systems, or organizing your spices. Taking time, saves time. Reminds me of the old saying: *a stitch in time saves nine.*

○ **Keep a master "DO" list.** Things to do NOW, LATER, SOMEDAY, MAYBE NEVER. Capture your ideas, worries and dreams on paper. There are many benefits to this habit; it reduces worry, makes dreams more likely to come true, and keeps your thoughts in a safe place that doesn't occupy brain space. Keep idea capturing notepads handy and transfer the important ideas to your master list or the relevant project file.

○ **Use the old-fashioned way.** After wasting what felt like an eternity going to my computer address book to look up contact info and usernames for websites I decided to get an old-fashioned, tried and true Rolodex to put beside my desk. I find it so much faster to reach over to my Rolodex to look up information than getting into my electronic address books. Plus, those Rolodex cards are really handy to keep in your wallet for capturing information. I guess that's why they are still around after all these years!

○ **Use index cards:** Index (or Rolodex) cards are super handy for putting in a wallet or pocket. You can use them for information about your day, shopping lists, contact info., or notes.

○ **Back up your computer!** I remember a friend telling me what her computer technician said to her after she lost all the data on her computer ~ there are those who back up their computers and those who will. This is one lesson you don't want to learn the hard way! Sometimes when I'm working on an important document I email it to myself, 'just in case' and leave it on my internet server until I don't need it anymore.

○ **Be a good delegator.** Learn when and how to delegate effectively. Clearly identify expectations, teach how if necessary, don't micro-manage, give sincere recognition for a job well-done and thoughtful coaching when improvement is needed.

○ **Use the Magical Manila File Folder.** Speaking of the old-fashioned way, file folders are an amazing, inexpensive organizing tool. You don't even need a filing cabinet for storage, an inexpensive file box will do. As soon as I start collecting papers on a topic I reach for a file

MAKE TIME YOUR FRIEND

folder and label it alphabetically. Mine are labelled, decorated, doodled on, have key phone numbers and information written all over them.

○ **About the Magical Manila File Folder.** Over the Christmas holidays, our family uses file folders to help plan for the new year. We get out the file folder for the previous year, and make one up for the New Year. We talk about the highlights of the previous year, and we put our 8 ½ by 11 calendar from the current year in the file, as a keepsake. We talk about what to do more of, what to do less of in the up-coming year. We remind ourselves of goals, key dates and standing commitments, like lacrosse season, and we come up with a plan. We write our main ideas on the front of the file folder. Then we get out our new year calendar and schedule in holidays, important dates, etc. We keep the file folder with ideas in our handy reference spot, and also use it for keepsakes.

○ **Keep key project files and reference information in a desktop file holder in a handy spot.** Keeping your key files in plain view helps; make things happen, control paper, meet project and other important deadlines, and saves time looking for lost paper. When no longer in use either recycle these files and their contents or add them to their appropriate spot in your alphabetical filing system. Sweet ☺

○ **Use plastic presentation folders and photo books.** Although I try to minimize the use of plastics, the simple book-style presentation folders are handy to organize frequently used material. Small plastic photo albums are also great, plus they are pocket-sized. These are especially useful for travelling as they hold up in damp conditions, and even fit in a passport holder so you have a back up of reservation, contact and other important travel info.

○ **Make the most of magical moments.** I remember talking to a friend once on her son's birthday and she was disappointed because she hadn't had time to plan something special. I suggested if it was a nice evening to lie in the backyard on a blanket and look at the stars. She called me the next day to thank me and tell me how wonderful an idea that was. There's nothing like a simple magical moment courtesy of Mother Nature. Often it's when we stop trying so hard that magical things happen.

○ **Take a Day to "Get Back on Track!"** This is a day that you take when you feel things are spinning out of control. Some call it a **STOP day**, or a day to get their affairs in order. Make an executive decision to clear your schedule or seize a day (like a snowy day when the roads are bad and you decide if's safer not to go out anyway) and use it for cleaning, tackling a project, planning or organizing, or even just to kick back and relax.

○ **Don't worry if your socks don't match.** Seriously. Wear mis-matched socks, as long as they are in the same colour family, and even if they aren't. This saves time, and money, and can be a really good conversation starter. **About those single socks.** They can make great cleaning rags or .....

Get in the groove:

○ **Multi-tasking is out and sequencing is "in."** There's a growing body of research that shows that multi-tasking is not beneficial, either to the person using that strategy or to getting the task done. **Sequencing tasks can make a big difference.** Become conscious of the order of your activities. For example, if I sit down to work before starting a load of dishes or laundry I regret it later. Taking the time up-front means those wonderful home appliances, for which I am very grateful, do chores while I work. Another example is placing an important call first thing in the morning so that there is plenty of time to try again or wait for a call-back.

○ **Find your rhythm:** Think about the best time to get things done based on your energy level. Pay attention to your natural rhythm ~ *are you energetic and creative in the morning and less so in the afternoon or evening?* Use your most energetic time to do your most important work or accomplish important tasks, and your less energetic times for routine activities.

○ **Build momentum:** Some days it seems easy to get stuff done. I love these days. I get one thing done, and get excited about the next thing I can get done and the satisfaction of getting things done fuels me to do more.

○ **Set the clock a few minutes fast.** My family hates it when I do this but it works to keep us on time, and helps keep my stress level low compared to when I'm rushing or worried about being late.

○ **Synchronicity.** Plan for and take advantage of gifts of time and coincidence. Pay attention to opportunities that present themselves. You have time to spare and you're right by a shop that has things you need. So you duck into the shop, get what you need, shopping done! Or, be prepared for a wait. I made edits to this workbook while waiting at the orthodontist (the bill was a good motivator)!

○ **Make it a game:** Set a timer or a deadline, and see how quickly things get done. Accomplish the number 1 priority, Take 5 and then tackle the next item. The two-minute rule works great for this, do one thing that takes two minutes and move on to the next, and the next, and…. Remember to TAKE 5!

○ **Make believe:** Pretend that you are going on vacation or that you've invited house guests to stay. These two tricks help me accomplish tasks at lightning speed.

○ **Use reminder bands.** Reminder bands are very popular these days and I think they are a fun way to remind you of a behaviour change you want to make or commitments you've made.

○ **Lower expectations.** Sometimes, it's just not possible to get it all done, especially if your standards are higher than required for the work to be done.

MAKE TIME YOUR FRIEND

Keep things tidy:

○ **Reduce.** It's easier to keep things tidy if you have less stuff! Before buying an item consider whether it's a want or something you really need. Try not to buy things you don't need.

○ **Put stuff back where you found it.** It's just as easy to put an item "back" in a drawer as "back" on a counter or desktop. This method only works if everything has a place…

○ **A place for everything and everything in it's place.** If there is a pattern to what's piling up in your space such as papers, it's a sign that you may need a system or place for that item. This could also be a sign that you need to de-clutter.

○ **Leave things the same or better than you found them.** I learned this important life lesson from our guide on a kayaking and wilderness camping excursion.

○ **The Magical Manila File Folder.** Make files rather than piles, see tip above.

○ **Maintain Home Base and establish a "baseline."** You can use this at home or at the office. Having things tidy and organized has a lot of benefits. Being organized usually makes us feel better, plus it saves time spent looking for things. It can even save money, not purchasing items you already have but just can't find. Find out how to establish a baseline in this book.

○ **Have a regular clean-up time in mind.** Think of a time during your week where you could most conveniently fit in a clean-up time, and try and make it a habit. Involve family members, and think of ways to make it fun, by putting a time limit on clean-up, for example. Or, agree to spend 15 minutes tidying before watching a movie or playing a game. You can be flexible about the 'clean-up time' but having a time in mind is more likely to make it happen. In Chapter 9, you can find a Housecleaning Fortune Teller to help make it fun.

○ **For a quick tidy-up.** Scan your space and think: what is one thing I could *quickly or easily* do that would make this space look better? Do that. If you have time to spare, repeat.

○ **De-clutter.** Regular de-cluttering keeps things tidy and can also turn up unexpected gifts. A purge of the too small clothes in one child's room results in a gift of 'barely used' clothes for another child. A purge of my husband's art area reveals the perfect bathroom organizer. I probably should have asked if I could re-locate it, but he hasn't even noticed yet!

○ **Keep up with the laundry.** Think about what it takes to keep up with your laundry and make it part of your daily or weekly plan, otherwise it can become overwhelming.

> *The laundry, the laundry, it's driving me insane!*
> *If I see another load of laundry,*
> *I think I'll stuff it down the drain!*
>
> Charlotte Diamond, Children's performer

Change your relationship with time:

○ **Be mindful.** Notice what's not working, like you're always looking for your keys! And, pay attention to what's working. Make small changes that make life easier. Smile at your cleverness. ☺ This builds positive momentum and creates a ripple effect.

○ **Keep a healthy pace with time and strike a balance between fast and slow.** Carl Honoré says 'Slow' is a way of being.[10] Further, he emphasizes: *"the Slow philosophy can be summed up in a single word: balance. Be fast when it makes sense to be fast, and be slow when slowness is called for."* For instance, *be slow,* when spending time with family and friends.

○ **Keep a list of things you've already done as well as those you want to do.** There's lots of talk about keeping *a life list of things to do.* I suggest keeping a list of the *great stuff we've already done.* Remembering, and being grateful for great experiences we've already had, and goals accomplished, helps keep things in perspective.

○ **Cut yourself some slack and lower expectations.** We don't have to be perfect all the time. *"If you're gonna play the game …you gotta learn to play it right, you've got to know when to hold 'em, know when to fold 'em, know when to walk away, and know when to run."* [11]

○ **Take 5.** Remember to Take 5 for fun and healthy work-life breaks and to reward yourself, or others, for a job well-done.

○ **Don't be afraid to do nothing at all.** It almost seems as though it has become a status symbol to have a busy schedule. Un-scheduled time leaves a bit of elasticity and give in the system to deal with unexpected things that come up, and time to kick back and reflect.

○ **Trust your brain to come up with solutions.** There has been much research to show that studying the night before an exam, after you've had a chance to 'sleep' on the material enhances test performance, or that upon awakening a solution to a problem will often present itself. A recent article in *Discover* magazine on The Brain,[12] suggests *"letting your attention wander may be the best way to set goals, make discoveries, and live a balanced life"*, although they do warn *"if you're pondering where you'll be in five years as you drive through a busy intersection, you may not be around in five years to find out."*

> *…the mind has powers that allow us to go beyond*
> *our habitual way of being, and beyond what we think is possible.*
> Joseph Jaworski, author, *Synchronicity.*

---

[10] Honore, Carl. 2004. *In Praise of Slow. How a Worldwide Movement is Challenging the Cult of Speed.*

[11] Kenny Rogers, Song, *The Gambler.*

[12] Zimmer, Carl. *Discover: The Brain.* Mindless, (Fall 2010). pg 64.

MAKE TIME YOUR FRIEND

- Let Google do the searching for you and deliver results to your inbox. Set a few key weekly ~ I don't recommend daily ~ Google alerts. Quickly scan the results and limit yourself to looking at the 2 or 3 most interesting and/or credible items. When your time limit is up, stop!

- Watch the Robin Williams Movie, 'RV', for laughs and inspiration to turn electronics off.

- If your friends and family call you Google, or you can't be dragged away from the computer without a fuss you might want to read this:
http://www.minddisorders.com/Flu-Inv/Internet-addiction-disorder.html

- I was stressing because my sons were spending too much time on electronics. So I asked myself "why?" I realized that the weather was not great 'outside' weather, and they were busted up from sports injuries and were taking it easy. So, I put our chess set in a prominent place. One small change, many positive results.

DEALING WITH INTERNET AND INFORMATION OVERLOAD

Are you spending too much time on the internet, chatting with friends, or chasing one link after the next, in search of information? It's not really a surprise that a growing body of research suggests this has negative implications for our brains, health, relationships and balance.

Step 1: Think about it!

Pause and think about how much time you are spending on the internet. Consider whether this is interfering with your relationships or other goals such as spending time with family, exercising, or completing an assignment. If yes, the steps below will help you develop some guidelines for internet use.

Step 2: Create and use an information filter.

Limit your topics. Decide on your current top 3 - 5 need-to-know topics or interests. Don't stray or minutes will turn into hours!

Bookmark the best sites. Identify the most credible sites for the information you're seeking. Make these sites your favourites and forget about others.

Unless you're working on a PhD the reality is that most of what we really need to know can be obtained from a few reliable sites. If you find yourself heading down the slippery slope, chasing a path of links and leads, consider whether you are getting any new or worthwhile information. *Ask: what else could I be doing with my time?*

Step 3: Take control.

Set time limits. Limit your internet time and decide when to call it quits. I know it's hard when the internet really is Orwellian. "IT" is a link to our friends and family, knows where we live, knows what we like to read, knows what we like to buy and what we are interested in, *and* IT tempts with offers like *'you might be interested in this….'*

Make the plan easy. For example: fifteen minutes after coffee break then back to work; electronics-free Sunday, or evenings after 8 pm; or whatever will work for you! Using electronics before bedtime interferes with our ability to fall asleep anyway, all the more reason to have computer free evenings. Remembering slogans can help make your plan easy, like "Unplug and Play" a concept promoted by ABC Life Literacy Canada, or "disconnect to connect."

Remember to Take 5. When sitting at the computer for long periods remember to take healthy mini-breaks. Look away from the screen, stand up and stretch, get up for a drink of water or tea, or engage in a face-to-face chat with family and friends.

INFORMATION OVERLOAD

A DAY THAT WORKS

Think about the ingredients in a recipe for *'a day that works'* for you. *What does that look like?* It's helpful to establish a general routine that keeps your work-life organized, in balance, and consistent with your priorities and goals. It's not realistic to think everyday will go as planned. So, think of this routine more like guidelines.

Make up your recipe for a day that works.

List some of the ingredients in your recipe for *a day that works*, then try it out, re-think it, and keep refining it, until it works for you. Think about the **Take 5** activities you can include ~ these are healthy work-life breaks that you enjoy and can easily fit into your day. Here's an example of how this could look.

SAMPLE:

Ingredient list:	My **Take 5** activity ideas:
AM:	O Go for a walk! No matter how short.
O Up early, so the morning isn't rushed, and there's time to listen to CBC am. ☺	O Deep Breathing.
O Start a load of laundry, so it's finished before leaving the house.	O Listen to music.
O A good cup of coffee, breakfast, then make lunches.	O Drink more water & tea.
O Confirm dinner plan.	O Refresh my face with cold water.
O Accomplish my number 1 priority!	O Talk with a friend.
PM:	O Read.
O A healthy family dinner.	O Knit a few rows.
O Early shut down of electronics.	O Play a short game.
O Review of calendar for the next day.	O Have a warm bath.
O Clothes and items for the morning ready.	O Be grateful for 5 things.
O Main rooms, especially kitchen, and desk tidied.	
Do something active everyday!	More about TAKE 5 later.

What's Your Recipe for a Day that Works?

Ingredient list:	My Take 5 activity ideas:

In an ideal world our days would be characterized by a sense of *flow and balance* where you move through your day in a comfortable rhythm. The start of the day sets your path. Start off with a drink of fresh water and the *splash and flow* of cold water over your face. [13]

> *Everyone has in his own home a Fountain of Youth*
> *in his basin of cold water on a morning bursting with energy....*
> *Fresh water awakens and gives youth to one's face,*
> *that place where a man sees himself growing old*
> *and where he would like to keep others from seeing him age!*
> *But fresh water does not rejuvenate our faces for others*
> *so much as for ourselves. Beneath the awakened brow*
> *gleams a new eye. Fresh water puts fire back in the eye.*
>
> Gaston Bachelard, French philosopher

---

[13] **Be grateful** if you have fresh drinking water in your home, many do not. Fresh water is a precious gift ~ that may even prevent wrinkles if you read between the lines of this quote by: Bachelard, Gaston. 1942. *Water and Dreams.* Read more on the concept of 'Flow' by: Csikszentmihalyi, Mihalyi. 1997. *Finding Flow*. Basic Books. New York.

A WEEK THAT WORKS

Your calendar, or planner is your basic planning tool and it's really important to choose one that fits your work, your life and your personal style. Regardless of the type of planner you use I recommend it includes a weekly overview.

Step 1: Make up a calendar that gives you an overview of your typical week.

Make up a week at a glance calendar like the one provided over. Or, if you use your computer calendar you can print one off from your computer. Write out what your typical week looks like. This doesn't have to be perfect, just get a sense of your schedule of re-occurring activities: work, school, commuting times, family and friends time, exercise, time for errands and chores, such as housecleaning, planning and organizing, grocery shopping, community service, and downtime.

Step 2: Think about it.

Now, look at the calendar and think about your typical week. *How do you feel during the week? Do you feel like you are always rushing? Are you exhausted at the end of the day or week? Are the basics attended to; such as health, family, home maintenance, safety and financial matters?*

Step 3: Keep it simple.

Establish a weekly schedule and routines. Note that this doesn't mean you can't switch things up once in a while!

At our house during winter: Friday is homemade pizza night; Saturday is pancake day; weekends are usually for sport activities or family time. We try not to schedule work-related travel on Mondays or Fridays, and we build down time into our calendar ~ to rejuvenate, get our house back in order or do something spontaneous.

Step 4: If you are overcommitted, de-clutter your calendar.

Decide if your schedule is sustainable given your current time, energy and financial resources. If not, have a serious look at whether it's time to de-clutter your calendar. *"Hoarding"* life experiences can be just as problematic as hoarding stuff. Ideas for de-cluttering your calendar include activity free days and/or evenings.

Step 5: Keep your weekly schedule and a monthly calendar in view.

Having a visible weekly and monthly calendar serves as one place to collect all important information and helps minimize conflict and stress by reducing rushing, missed appointments, over-booking, etc. I like an 8 ½ by 11 calendar printed on acid-free paper. At the end of the year this can easily be tucked in a standard file folder as a memory keeper. That's sweet. ☺

- Highlight your top 3-5 goals or action/steps for the week on your weekly calendar.

- Use a weekly menu planner to save time, money and the stress of *"what's for dinner?"* To really simplify things keep the recipes you use most frequently handy. For example, we often have homemade pizza, so the dough recipe is taped to the inside of a kitchen cupboard. Find a weekly menu planner and shopping list in this book and a full colour version at the WorkLife Café website.

- Do a weekly review, ideally Friday, to ensure that there are no surprises in the upcoming week.

- When using a monthly calendar, use the space at the end of the month to note commitments early in the next month. For example, an important birthday or milestone that requires some advance planning. If these dates fall in the first week of a month they often get missed. You can download a WorkLife Café monthly calendar from the WorkLife Café website.

- **Use WorkLife Wednesday as a balance check day**. Use the balance check exercise in this book and think about the forces that are pushing and pulling you out of balance. Make adjustments, if necessary. You can use the extra copies of the (Un) Balancing Forces exercise in this workbook, or download them at the WorkLife Café.

WORKLIFE, CAFE | WEEKLY WORKLIFE PLANNER

Week of _____ **Year** _____

	MONDAY	TUESDAY	WORKLIFE WEDNESDAY	THURSDAY	FRIDAY	SATURDAY	SUNDAY
MORNING							
AFTERNOON							
EVENING							

WORKLIFE, CAFE

Weekly Meal Planner & SHOPPING LIST

DAY	Breakfast	Lunch	Dinner	Recipe Source
Monday				
Tuesday				
Wednesday				
Thursday				
Friday				
Saturday				
Sunday				

SHOPPING LIST

TIP) It helps to organize your shopping list so it matches the flow of the store where you shop.

© WorkLife Cafe are all rights reserved. This template is for personal use only.

HABITS THAT WORK ~ DEVELOP A NEW POSITIVE HABIT

Positive habits contribute to work-life success and wellbeing. *"If you adopt the right lifestyle... chances are you may live up to a decade longer."* [14] Think of a positive habit to develop that would enhance your work-life balance and wellbeing.

The habit I'm working on developing.

intend to:

Advantages of developing this habit: [15]	Potential disadvantages or challenges:
An indicator of your change readiness is having a longer list of advantages, than disadvantages.	
What is needed to be successful?	**Ideas for overcoming challenges:**
Think of resources needed such as; time, supplies, $. *Tip:* Keep track to stay on track!	Be creative and resourceful about overcoming challenges; ask *what if I ....?* You can use a Mind Map to help brainstorm ideas.
My Reward ☺	**Results and Observations:**

---

[14] Buettner, Dan. Nov. 2005. The Secrets of Living Longer. *National Geographic.*

[15] Prochaska, Jo et al. 1994. *Changing for Good. The revolutionary program that explains the six stages of change and teaches you how to free yourself from bad habits.*

HABITS THAT WORK ~ KEEP TRACK TO STAY ON TRACK

A common saying is '*you can only improve what gets measured*.' So, ensure your goal is specific, measureable and achievable. Then, **keep track to stay on track**. Say you're planning to Take 5 everyday, or prepare a healthy family dinner 6 nights a week, then keep track.

Step 1: What am I working on?

Step 2: How am I doing?

You can use the charts on the following pages to keep track of how you're doing.

- Research says it takes 21 to 30 days to develop a new habit.

- Developing a new habit can take a few tries. You've heard the saying *"if at first you don't succeed, try and try again"*.

- Use something as a reminder of the new habit you are trying to develop, such as a sticker on your computer screen, a reminder wristband, a picture or post-it note.

- Writing and signing a certificate of commitment to your goal is helpful. An example of a commitment contract is in our Take 5 program, in Chapter 5.

- A *Complaint Free World* envisioned by Will Bowen, provides a reminder band *"to help people develop the habit to leave the toxic communication of complaining behind and experience an internal shift toward being more positive, hopeful and optimistic."* The website has a 21 day challenge and a counter for keeping track of complaint free days. People are finding the experience of being complaint free transformative: http://www.acomplaintfreeworld.org/

WORKLIFE CAFE | WEEKLY ACTIVITY PLANNER

Week of _____ **Year** _____

	MONDAY	TUESDAY	WEDNESDAY	THURSDAY	FRIDAY	SATURDAY	SUNDAY
MORNING	ACTIVITY _Go for a walk_ ✓	ACTIVITY ◯	ACTIVITY ◯	ACTIVITY ◯	ACTIVITY ◯	ACTIVITY ◯	ACTIVITY ◯
AFTERNOON	ACTIVITY ◯	ACTIVITY ◯	ACTIVITY ◯	ACTIVITY ◯	ACTIVITY ◯	ACTIVITY ◯	ACTIVITY ◯
EVENING	ACTIVITY ◯	ACTIVITY ◯	ACTIVITY ◯	ACTIVITY ◯	ACTIVITY ◯	ACTIVITY ◯	ACTIVITY ◯

BREATHE · 2 DRINK A GLASS · EXERCISE · 4 GO A WALK · MEDITATE · 1 PARTICIPATE · TAKE 5

worklifecafe.ca

© WorkLifeCafe.ca All rights reserved. This template is for personal use. PLEASE RECYCLE

WORKLIFE CAFÉ

MONTHLY ACTIVITY PLANNER

Month of _____

Year _____

MONDAY	TUESDAY	WEDNESDAY	THURSDAY	FRIDAY	SATURDAY	SUNDAY
ACTIVITY Go for a walk. ○✓	ACTIVITY ○	ACTIVITY ○	ACTIVITY ○	ACTIVITY ○	ACTIVITY ○	ACTIVITY ○
ACTIVITY ○	ACTIVITY ○	ACTIVITY ○	ACTIVITY ○	ACTIVITY ○	ACTIVITY ○	ACTIVITY ○
ACTIVITY ○	ACTIVITY ○	ACTIVITY ○	ACTIVITY ○	ACTIVITY ○	ACTIVITY ○	ACTIVITY ○
ACTIVITY ○	ACTIVITY ○	ACTIVITY ○	ACTIVITY ○	ACTIVITY ○	ACTIVITY ○	ACTIVITY ○
ACTIVITY ○	ACTIVITY ○	ACTIVITY ○	ACTIVITY ○	ACTIVITY ○	ACTIVITY ○	ACTIVITY ○

worklifecafé.ca

DECISIONS, DECISIONS

Having a few tools in your decision-making toolkit is helpful. For one, it helps avoid the *could of, would of, should have* lament, because you have more confidence that past decisions were well-thought out. Here's a few methods for making decisions.

Option 1: Use your WorkLife Framework and your intuition.

When you have a decision to make you can use the key questions related to your WorkLife Framework, developed in Chapter 2. Thinking through the impact of the decision will often help you point to a clear yes or no. For example, consider: *What impact will this decision have on my current goals and priorities such as: Family and Finances?* Sometimes it's not so easy to decide. For example, our current family framework includes family, finances and fun. Even though finances are important we decided to compromise finances for an extended family vacation. We decided that creating family memories and having fun was more important to us given the age of our family members and our life stage.

Sometimes your decisions can compromise what's important to you. Once you've thought through the impact of the decision you have to carefully decide if moving forward is worth the cost. Decide if you can live with the consequences. Feelings can be an important clue. *Always consider how the decision feels.*

Option 2: Rank choices.

Ranking can help you make choices when you've got a few options. Make a list of your choices and rank them numerically in order of preference. Keep crossing off the last choices on your list until you only have one left.

Option 3: Consider advantages and disadvantages.

This is the tried and true method of making decisions. List the advantages and disadvantages. Sometimes an obvious choice will emerge.

Option 4: Use 10-10-10.

This is a much simplified version of an idea from Suzy Welch, author of *10-10-10*.[16] When faced with a decision ask: *what will the consequences of my options be in the next 10 minutes? 10 months? 10 years?* The book is filled with examples that lead to a comprehensive understanding of how 10-10-10 works.

---

[16] Suzy Welch. *10-10-10. A Life Transforming Idea.* http://www.suzywelch101010.com

Option 5: Ask for help.

Do not hesitate to ask for help from family, friends and professionals when you have difficult decisions to make. Getting another, ideally objective opinion, can be helpful.

Option 6: Use a business case analysis.

Well, I can't sum this one up in 3 lines but in some cases a more complex analysis may be required for decision-making, such as a feasibility study or business case analysis. This is particularly important if the decision has significant financial or other risk. These analyses may include: an overview of the challenge or problem, the reason why a decision has to be made, research of all the important related factors like environmental trends, costs and benefits, options and recommendations.

Option 7: Develop and use key questions.

Develop and use key questions related to a decision you've already made to help you stay on track. Say your goal is saving up for a family vacation but you'd really like to purchase a new TV. You could develop a key question like *"how will this decision impact my saving for the family vacation?"*

Other key questions:

- *What's the worst thing that could happen?*
- *Can I go back on this decision?*
- *What happens if I just take the next action/step?*
- *Will this activity help me achieve my key goal of _____ ?*

DO NOT make important decisions when in a major crisis or life stage without careful **consideration. At these times it's best to get back to basics, and ask for help!**

> *There is a voice inside of you that whispers all day long. "I feel that this is right for me, I know that this is wrong." No teacher, preacher, parent, friend or wise man can decide what's right for you. Just listen to the voice that speaks inside of you.*
> Shell Silverstein, American poet.

Brainstorming Session
M**I**NDMAP

Name _____

Date _____

Remember to post in a visible spot!

References & Resources
- Mind Mapping idea from Tony Buzan
- Check out this link for more mind map inspiration
  www.mindmapinspiration.com

CONTINGENCY PLANNING

Life happens. Days just don't go as you planned. While it's not possible to plan for everything that can come up, it is helpful to anticipate and have a plan for contingencies.

Step 1: Identify challenges. Ask what if.......?

Think of things that could come up in your life. For example: a family member that lives far away needs help, your daycare arrangement falls through, a family member's cell phone is lost or stops working, your flight home is cancelled, there's a major snowstorm, or...

Possible Challenge	Contingency Plan and Action Steps

Step 2: Schedule action steps.

Schedule time in your calendar for action items required to put your contingency plan in place.

MAINTAIN HOME BASE

When we get too busy our 'space' can become a drop off zone; cluttered, untidy and a source of stress. Establish a baseline for your home base (or office) and make a plan to maintain it.

Step 1: Assess the situation.

Consider the big picture. Look around your space and jot down some thoughts about the following: *What does my space look like right now? How does it make me feel? When I look around am I overwhelmed by stuff and undone chores? Is it comfortable to be in? Is it functional?*

Step 2: Decide on a "baseline".

I think most of us have already intuitively established an office or housekeeping 'baseline'. I think of this as how I want my space to look and feel on a day-to-day basis so that it is comfortable to be in rather than a source of stress. To help you decide on a baseline become aware of when your space feels comfortable to be in. Think about how it feels. Keep this picture in your mind as the baseline. This may not be the way you want your space to look and feel at its best, it's the more realistic picture of how a lived in space feels and looks.

Scan your space on a regular basis. When the baseline is crossed, and you've passed the level of untidiness you can tolerate, it's time to take other stuff off the list and make finding a time to clean-up the number 1 priority! Once you have this system in place it may also give you a sense of how long it takes you to get things back to the way you like them. If a major clean-up or de-cluttering is necessary check out the suggestions in this book.

Step 3: Make a home maintenance plan.

Identify systems and routines to keep your office or home the way you like it, such as a regular weekly clean-up time.

- It's easier to keep things tidy if you have less stuff!

GET ORGANIZED

There seems to be a lot of talk these days about the benefits of organizing and simplifying your work and life. Here are some ideas to get you started.

Step 1: Establish systems and routines.

"Automate or Simplify" tasks and activities such as menu planning, filing and tidying. While it may seem boring, systems and routines can help you save time, money and reduce stress. Jot down a few thoughts about what aspects of your work-life might be improved if you established the right system or routine. *Are you spending too much time searching for reference material, warranties, or receipts? Are you missing appointments, events or deadlines?* If you answered yes to any of these questions here are two ideas that might help.

Step 2: Begin with a filing and calendar system.

Create and Use An Alphabetical Filing System.

Make files not piles! This is no time for perfection, just get started putting a filing system in place. All you need is inexpensive cardboard bankers boxes, simple manila file folders, and a felt pen. After you set up the initial system, which can take a while, maintenance should require only a few minutes a day. Keep the files you use most often close at hand or chances are you won't use them at all. It's also important to use a good filing method for your computer files.

Choose and Use A Calendar System that matches your needs.

Find a calendar that you will use and consult on a daily basis to record appointments, plan and schedule your time. There are endless choices. Be patient, it may take you a while to find the format that works best for you. Essentials for me are a week overview and space to write out my top 3-5 priorities and make a few other notes.

References & Resources

- The David Allen Co. website offers free downloads on how to establish an alphabetical filing system (and many more excellent tip sheets on organizing.)
  https://secure.davidco.com/store/catalog/Free-Articles-p-1-c-254.php

- Randy Pausch, Ph.D. described the virtues of a simple alphabetical filing system and calendars in his ~ Time Management Lecture (1 hour), inspiring and informative.
  http://download.srv.cs.cmu.edu/~pausch/

- I like Polestar paper calendars that promote balance, especially their business calendar.
  http://www.polestarcalendars.com/index.php

SPRING CLEAN ~ ANYTIME

A clean and organized space has so many work-life benefits. Being organized saves time and reduces stress plus a tidy space is generally more inviting. All good! People often spring clean, once a year, but you can do it anytime.

Step 1: Think about it.

For the 'big clean', the best plan is to pick a time and jump in. But, sometimes it's good to think about the big picture first.

Scan and think about your living and/or office space. *What needs to be done to clean or clear up your space to make it more inviting and functional?* Make some notes. This doesn't have to be perfect.

Step 2: Identify the key steps.

List the key steps to clean-up and clear up that fit your time, capability and money budget. If you don't have adequate resources for 'the big clean', then do what you can. Keep your list handy for another time.

Step 3: Schedule time, gather your supplies and get started.

Schedule a time for your cleaning date. Also, list and gather necessary supplies.

Tip: Don't make this a big project unless you have all the resources. If you are overwhelmed by clutter I highly recommend FlyLady.net, link below.

Step 4: Remember to Take 5 for breaks and Reward Yourself.

References and Resources
- Find FlyLady's cleaning plan at: http://www.flylady.net/pages/ TableOfContents.asp then FLYing Lessons, Fly Lady's Crisis Cleaning
- Green cleaning recipes http://www.squidoo.com/GreenCleaningRecipes

Sample supplies list:
- A plan!
- Boxes or bags for: recycling, donating, distributing (items later to their proper homes), tossing, selling, sorting and thinking about.
- Cleaning products. Liquid soap, baking soda, vinegar and lemon juice can be used for many cleaning jobs and are environmentally friendly.

DE-CLUTTER

There's a lot of talk about de-cluttering these days. *(I realize it's ironic that we live in a society where a major concern for many people is having too much stuff!)* There are many excellent books and websites providing advice on de-cluttering. The following is a highly condensed version on the art of de-cluttering.

Step 1: Re-think and reduce.

Reducing is the key to eliminating clutter. Think twice about buying something you don't need, or before printing an email or computer information.

Step 2: Make a de-cluttering kit.

A de-cluttering kit is a key tool if you're doing a large purge. Even better, if you keep a de-cluttering kit made up all the time you may avoid getting to the purging stage.

You can use re-useable Kraft bags or boxes and label them:

- **Donate to _____,**
- **Recycle,**
- **Repair,**
- **Decide by _____, (for items your not sure about)**
- **Rags,**
- **Distribute (to their proper place.)**

(If you're doing a big de-cluttering you will probably also need a garbage bag.)

Step 3: Use the secret question to de-clutter.

If you come across an item that you Do Not Love, Need and/or Use Frequently then ask the Secret question: *Is this something I can easily replace if wanted or needed again?*

EASILY = it's not expensive, it's not family memorabilia or an irreplaceable keepsake, it's easy to find again. For example, the *"I've seen better days white t-shirt?"* If you ask the secret question and the answer is yes, then put the item in one of your labelled bags.

I think de-cluttering works best if it's a habit. Be mindful. If you're folding laundry and you think *'this t-shirt has seen better days'* then put it in the rag or donate bag or box. (Rags can also be donated, check in your local recycling directory.)

References & Resources

- FlyLady.net providing light-hearted information to help de-clutter www.flylady.net

DE-CLUTTER TOOL

(Copy, de-clutter and repeat as necessary)

If you come across an item that you Do Not Love, Need and/or Use Frequently then ask the Secret question: *Is this something I can EASILY replace if needed or wanted again?*

EASILY = it's not expensive, it's not family memorabilia or an irreplaceable keepsake, it's easy to find again.

If the answer to this question is YES, then put the item in a container labelled with one of the following labels:

(If you're doing a big de-clutter you will probably also need a garbage bag.)

Donate to:	Recycle:
Repair:	Decide by:
Rags:	Distribute:

CHAPTER 4:
SUSTAIN YOURSELF

This chapter provides some ideas and tools to help you maintain a happier and healthier balance between work and life, re-fuel, and rejuvenate.

A basic premise of this workbook is TAKE 5 and this chapter provides TAKE 5 ideas for you.

BREATHE DEEP ~ (5x5)

Life Happens! No matter how hard we try to gain control over day-to-day activities, unexpected things come up that cause stress. Chronic stress is not good for us. Something we can learn and practice to help alleviate the negative effects of stress, is to **breathe deep.** You can also get in the habit of using this breathing exercise as a balance check.

While I have been aware of the benefits of deep (belly) breathing, it was not until I read *The UltraMind Solution* by Dr. Mark Hyman, that I truly understood how and why belly breathing is so important. His book is jam packed with information. The following is a much simplified overview of the information about deep breathing.[17]

While some stress in our lives is necessary, a repeated pattern of stressful incidents is not healthy, as this can increase cortisol levels that contribute to hypertension, compromise our immune system, and damage our brain. Learning to activate the vagus nerve triggers the relaxation response *"necessary for your body to heal, repair, and renew".*

The vagus nerve, *"flows from your brain through your neck, right into your chest, and through your diaphragm. So when you take a deep breath and relax and expand your diaphragm, your vagus nerve is stimulated, you instantly turn on the parasympathetic nervous system, your cortisol levels are reduced, and your brain heals. This whole experience is called the relaxation response."* Meditation also activates the vagus nerve.

Step 1: Try this, and feel your tension float away...

Take 5
Relax your posture and place your hands on your softened belly.

"Take a deep breath into your belly to the count of five,
pause for one second,
then breathe out slowly to the count of five.
Keep your belly soft."

Repeat 5 times.

---

[17] All information appearing in quotations here is from Hyman, M. 2009. *The UltraMind Solution*, pg. 278. Dr. Hyman also credits James, Gordon, M.D. of the Center for Mind-Body Medicine (www.cmbm.org) for Soft-Belly Breathing.

According to Dr. Hyman, this breathing exercise has potential to be transformative for our health and wellbeing. His advice: *"During the [UltraMind] program try doing it five times a day. Do it when you wake up, before you go to bed, and when you sit down to each meal. Your life will change."*

Given the mounting evidence indicating chronic stress may literally be *"killing us"* it can only be helpful to learn and incorporate techniques such as deep breathing to activate our relaxation response. [18]

Step 2: Plan to include deep breathing in your day.

What are your ideas for incorporating this breathing technique into your day?

When I use this breathing exercise I instantly feel my stress level subside. I use it often when driving as I notice myself tensing up sometimes when I listen to the news or think about the traffic.

BANISH **Automatic Negative Thoughts (A.N.T.s)** using this deep breathing exercise. I think it would work! ANTs is a term used to describe a pattern or cycle of negative thinking or worry that can increase negativity, anxiety and cause stress.[19]

Here's an idea. When you notice a negative thought just think **N.G.T ~ Not Going There!** and change your focus to your breath ~ breathe deep. ☺

---

[18] *The Globe and Mail*, October 30, 2010. A12-13. Stress: *How your busy life is killing you.* Reports readers surveyed reported they experienced 14 stressful incidents a day.

[19] Learn more about ANTs in *Change Your Brain, Change Your Life*. Daniel G. Amen, MD.

- When doing the research for 'Get Connected!', next, I learned Sardinians from Italy partly owe their longevity to factors such as: good genes; family first; enjoying red wine made from Cannonau grapes in moderation; and eating Pecorino cheese made from sheep's milk high in Omega 3 fats. Seems like one way to enhance your wellbeing may be to get together with family and friends for *wine (or grape juice) and cheese*. How fun! [20]

- If you're short on time or funds you can provide the place and have guests bring the wine, or grape juice, and cheese. Just to make sure this was a worthwhile idea I splurged and tested Crotonese cheese recommended by our local Italian deli and Agriolas Costera, Cannonau di Sardegna wine. Nice.

---

[20] Buettner, Dan. Nov. 2005. The Secrets of Living Longer. *National Geographic.* National Geographic Society. Washington D.C. According to this article Cannonau grapes from the 'mountainous part of Sardinia contain two to three times as much of a component found in other wines that may prevent cardiovascular disease.'

GET CONNECTED! ~ THE ROSETO EFFECT

Research shows connection with family and friends contributes to better health, longevity and stronger families. **So, get connected!**

The Roseto Effect and why it matters to you.

Medical researchers were drawn to study a close-knit Italian-American community in Roseto, Pennsylvania by a bewildering statistic: in defiance of medical logic, Rosetans died of heart attacks at a rate of only half of the rest of America. Their research confirmed the importance of social networks in health and longevity.

So, Get Connected! You could live longer, plus it's more FUN!

Take 5 to Reconnect after being apart: At the end of the work day or being apart, spend time sitting together, with or without a lot of talking, this will help you reconnect and re-establish your family rhythm.

Make a date: Talk to a neighbour; call a friend to chat or make a date to do something together; plan a walk, a game or a movie night; volunteer; or sign up for that course you've always wanted to take.

Share a meal: Invite people over for a potluck or a one-pot dinner. Keep things informal and fun. It's more likely to happen that way.

When it comes to family, make an extra effort to share a family meal. There is a growing body of research about the many benefits of family mealtime.

> *....there is something about a shared meal*
> *...that anchors a family even on nights when the food is fast*
> *and the talk cheap and everyone has someplace else they'd rather be.*
> *And on those evenings when the mood is right and the family lingers,*
> *caught up in an idea or an argument explored in a shared safe place*
> *where no one is stupid or shy or ashamed, you get a glimpse of the power*
> *of this habit and why social scientists say such communion acts as*
> *a kind of vaccine, protecting kids from all manner of harm.* [21]
> 'The Magic of the Family Meal', Nancy Gibbs

[21] *The Magic of the Family Meal,* Nancy Gibbs, Time.com, Sunday, Jun. 04, 2006
http://alturl.com/y7ujy

Step 1: Write down your ideas to get and stay connected.

```

```

Step 2: Take the next step.

In your calendar write down your next action/step.

For example, call _____ and invite them to _____ .

In our world, we have to be particularly vigilant to nurture connection, community and meaning, because so many forces conspire to distract us from ourselves.
Mark Hyman, M.D. *The UltraMind Solution.*

References and Resources:

- Reconnecting idea from: Biddulph, Steve. 2004. *The Secrets of Happy Parents.* Thorsons: Wellingborough

- Read more about the **Roseto Effect** and the importance of social networks in health and longevity at http://www.uic.edu/classes/osci/osci590/14_2_The_Roseto_Effect.htm

- Buettner, Dan. Nov. 2005. The Secrets of Living Longer. *National Geographic.* National Geographic Society. Washington D.C. Pg. 13.

MEDITATE ~ MY WAY

Meditation is good for our health, helping us to manage our stress and give our minds, body and spirit, a much needed rest. The great news is that any activity that helps you lose track of time, really be in the moment, or distract you from worrisome thoughts can be beneficial. These activities also contribute to our happiness.

List your favourite "meditative" activities.

Take 5 and think about activities that are calming, or that you enjoy so much that you are totally immersed in the activity, lose track of time, and 'find flow'. Mihaly Csikszentmihalyi, author of *Finding Flow* describes this as a sense of serenity that comes when your *"...heart, will and mind are on the same page."* List some activities that help to distract and relax you here:

O		O
O	MED TATE	O
O	*WORKLIFECAFE.CA*	O
O		O
What calming activity could you most easily include in your day? And how?		

Ideas of activities that can be "meditative" by helping to distract and rejuvenate:

Walking, reading, listening to music, deep breathing, hobbies, playing an instrument, playing games, reading, having a bath, drawing, knitting, going to a concert, watching a sports event, hiking, fishing, water/skiing, swimming, sex, dancing, puzzles, canoeing, kayaking, gardening. Some people seek out water ~ creeks, brooks, springs, spas, pools, relaxing baths, showers, lakes and oceans ~ when they are stressed. Of course, yoga is an age old form of meditation. Obviously, for some of these activities you will need to dedicate more time than a few minutes. Note: Mihaly Csikszentmihalyi, author of *Finding Flow,* describes how people experience the powerful state of flow more while driving than in any other part of their lives!

Brainstorming Session
MINDMAP

Name _____

Date _____

Remember to post in a visible spot!

PLEASE RECYCLE

References & Resources
- Mind Mapping idea from Tony Buzan
- Check out this link for more mind map inspiration
  www.mindmapinspiration.com

NATURE EXPEDITION DAY

Plan a nature expedition or an outing that fills your soul, inspires you and helps you re-fuel. Go alone or go with friends to a favourite spot or explore unknown territory.

Where are going to go and what are you going to do?

Use the Mind Map provided to jot down some ideas. *Where would you like to go and what you would like to do? Will you include others?* Also think about your budget for this day.

What's in your backpack?

What will you take with you? You can use your Mind Map for your ideas.

Make it official.

Write down the date for your expedition, it's more likely to happen that way. Also write in your calendar anything else you need to do to make your expedition a success.

What's in it for you and others?

How do you think you will feel after your expedition? What are you most looking forward to? How do you think other people close to you will feel about your nature expedition? What do you think they will notice?

Remember Safety First! Make sure your plan is safe and you have notified an emergency contact of your plan. Get help from a knowledgeable source if necessary.

Want more info?

- Get inspiration for your nature outing from this web site that focuses on Canadian outdoor activities; http://www.outdooradventurecanada.com/index.html

- For a Basic Hiking and Picnic safety checklist ~ http://www.healthy-picnics.com/hiking_safety_checklist.html

- Some guidelines for organizers ~ http://www.voyageurtrail.ca/leaders.html

- What's in Your Backpack idea from a movie that makes you think about work-life balance "Up in the Air" starring George Clooney.

Brainstorming Session
MINDMAP

Name _____

Date _____

Remember to post in a visible spot!

PLEASE RECYCLE

References & Resources

• Mind Mapping idea from Tony Buzan
• Check out this link for more mind map inspiration
  www.mindmapinspiration.com

CHAPTER 5:
TAKE 5 PROGRAM

Take 5 is a basic premise of this book. Take 5 represents the idea that simple changes can make a big difference. Take 5 is intended to be an easy to remember reminder of the importance of taking healthy breaks and having a little fun. Sometimes we only have 5 minutes for a break, other times we have longer. The important thing is to get in the habit of taking positive steps towards a healthier balance and wellbeing ~ no matter how small the steps.

This chapter provides ideas for a **Take 5** program. Hopefully there is something here that works to help you incorporate Take 5 into your daily routine.

Great news! Beautiful colour copies of the exercises, planners and fun stuff in this Workbook are available **FREE** for one-year with your purchase of this book. Visit the WorkLife Café at http://www.worklifecafe.ca . Follow the link for Workbook Resources. On the sign in page type in the username: worklifecafe   password: take5 ~ all lower case.

TAKE 5 ~ FOR FUN AND BETTER HEALTH

When times are stressful it can be more important than ever to TAKE 5 for healthy breaks and to have a little fun. Often we only have a few minutes here or there to re-charge, but using those few minutes effectively can make a huge difference to our overall health and work-life quality.

Step 1: Find a quiet spot and brainstorm Take 5 ideas.

Use our handy Take 5 Mind Map on the next page. Write as many ideas as you can think of to help you re-energize and reduce stress. (You can refer to the previous chapter for ideas.) Also consider some of the benefits of taking fun and healthy breaks.

Step 2: Review and group your ideas by the time required.

If you used the Mind Map, your ideas will be grouped by the time needed for each activity; 5 minutes, 5 to 30 minutes, 30 minutes to a half day, 1/2 day or more. Note that some activities may fit in more than one category, like going for a walk. Walking is a great way to take a break no matter how long you walk. Be sure to include lots of ideas for short breaks as often that's all the time we have.

Step 3: Plan ahead to re-energize, reduce stress and improve your health.

Gather up the supplies you need for your activities, like walking shoes. Keep them handy, and then schedule breaks into your day. Feel like there's NO TIME!? Start with small breaks and notice how much better you feel. You'll soon be hooked!

Step 4: Post your ideas in a visible spot to inspire you to Take 5.

Taking fun and healthy breaks is good for you!

Step 5: Kick it up a notch by using our Take 5 Program. Read on...

CHECK WITH YOUR DOCTOR BEFORE STARTING ANY EXERCISE OR ACTIVITY PROGRAM

For Fun and Better Health

MINDMAP

My Mind Map of ideas for activities that help me laugh, recharge and reduce stress.

Take 5 to 30 Minutes

Take 5 Minutes

Take 30 Minutes to ½ Day

Take ½ Day or More

Having Fun is...

Name

Date

Remember to post in a visible spot!

References & Resources

- Mind Mapping idea from Tony Buzan
- Check out this link for more mind map inspiration
  www.mindmapinspiration.com

worklifecafé.ca

About Take 5.

Take 5 encourages taking small healthy breaks and putting a little bit more fun into your day to support a healthier work-lifestyle. Stress related illness and lack of physical activity are a big problem in our society. A lot of our stress and poor health is a result of long hours at work, sitting for extended periods of time, not eating wholesome foods, running ourselves ragged, not getting enough rest, not getting enough exercise, and spending too much time with technology as our friend.

Because so many of us are so busy and often sitting for long periods, developing the habit of taking healthy breaks can help us reduce stress, improve our balance and overall wellbeing. This has many spin off effects such as: improved health, more energy, feeling better about ourselves, and spending more time with family and friends by including them in activities.

A healthier balance contributes to a better overall quality of life.

Take 5 encourages momentum towards a healthier work-lifestyle. **Take 5** does not replace a regular exercise or healthy lifestyle program. The goal of **Take 5** is to promote a healthier balance, including regular healthy mini-breaks during your day as small steps on the path to a more active and healthy lifestyle, or a complement to an already active and healthy lifestyle.

Examples of small steps toward a healthier lifestyle include:

- taking a stretch break when sitting for long periods;
- having a glass of water or cup of tea instead of another cup of coffee; and,
- going for a short walk.

CHECK WITH YOUR DOCTOR BEFORE STARTING ANY EXERCISE OR ACTIVITY PROGRAM

Why Take 5?

Often we only have a few minutes here or there to recharge. Using those few minutes effectively can make a huge difference to our overall health and work-life quality.

How to Take 5.

You can easily incorporate **Take 5** into your day... at work, at home, or on the go.

One. Plan for Take 5 healthy mini-breaks throughout the day and use reminders.

Two. Look for opportunities to Take 5 throughout the day. For example: get off transit 1 stop before your usual stop or park farther away from your destination; take the stairs; if watching television exercise during commercial breaks; instead of another cup of coffee have a water or tea, or...

Three: Like it! If you choose activities you enjoy you are more likely to include them in your day.

Four: Make your Take 5 plan easy. Make it convenient, keep it simple, and start small. Small steps create momentum toward positive change and achieving larger goals.

Consider Your Take 5 Ideas.

Consider the ideas on your Mind Map that help you re-energize and reduce stress. Think about mixing it up a bit by including a variety of activities.

* For **Take 5** ideas and inspiration in a highly readable format I recommend: *You Don't Have to Go Home from Work Exhausted: A Program to Bring Joy, Energy, and Balance to Your Life*, by Anne McGee-Cooper.

Think about the benefits of Take 5.

*What would be the biggest benefit of **Take 5** for you?*

[ ]

Look over your Mind Map again and circle or highlight the activities you'd like to try over the next month. Note that some activities may fit in more than one group, like going for a walk. Walking is a great way to take a break no matter how long you walk.

Consider whether your ideas are realistic given your current commitments, time, health and resources. If you are also trying to enhance your work-life balance, consider how taking healthier breaks may help you achieve other goals and fulfill mind, body, spirit and emotional needs. For example, doing something ACTIVE with family and friends benefits you on many levels.

Now, plan a journey on the Take 5 Train.

I came across a little booklet called *"Waiting at the Station"* that I describe in more detail later. This is a story about how people can pass their whole lives waiting on the platform at the train station watching all the trains (opportunities) go by because they are afraid to get on the train as they are not quite sure of the destination or what the journey will be like.

The metaphor of a train is often used in North American culture. For example, people will say *"I'm off track"* or *"I need to get back on track."* This exercise can help you with your decision to get on the Take 5 activity train. As an added bonus it's fun!

You can make up a "goal" train to remind you of your **Take 5** plan. *Here's how:*

TAKE 5

Decide on your Take 5 goal,
~ your main reason for getting on the Take 5 Train.

What is your reason for taking the Take 5 activity train? Is it to manage stress, improve your work-life balance, feel better, walk more, lose weight, or …? Write your goal in the space below.

What are the action/steps for reaching your destination or goal?

Write your action/steps in the space below.

SAMPLE

GOAL: TO MANAGE STRESS

Action/steps:

• Take 5 walks a week
• Take 5 minutes at lunch everyday to practice relaxation exercises.
• Talk to a close friend about worries or concerns.

MY GOAL: _____

Action/steps:

•
•
•

Write your destination, in this case your **Take 5** goal, on the train engine. You can use the train cars to write down the action/steps required to reach your destination or goal. For example: Take 5 everyday; drink 8 glasses of water a day; go for a walk during lunch or coffee break. Whatever you think might work for you. The train only has two cars, so if you have more goals you'll just have to squish them on there like passengers on a train!

TAKE 5 ACTIVITY GOAL TRAIN

Make a note of any other things that might be important to; do, have or keep in mind along the journey to make it a success.

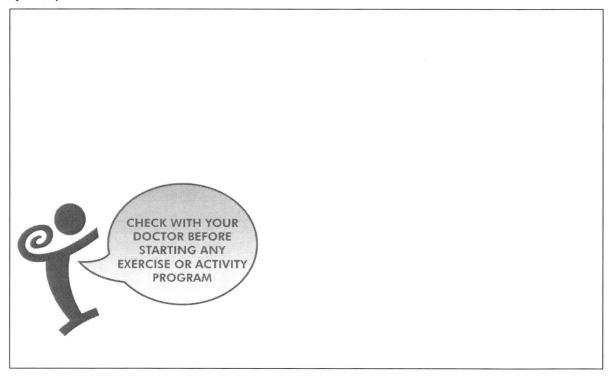

Set your mind to it!

Imagine yourself committing to taking action/steps towards a healthier balanced work-lifestyle; becoming more active, drinking more water, eating better, or whatever your goal is.

Ask yourself:

How will I think and feel about myself once I have created these new positive habits?

How will making positive changes that enhance my wellbeing impact me and my relationships?

CHECK WITH YOUR DOCTOR BEFORE STARTING ANY EXERCISE OR ACTIVITY PROGRAM

Gather supplies.

*Keep **Take 5** simple.* If possible, choose activities that use items you already have and that you can easily fit into your work-lifestyle. Gather up any supplies you need and keep them handy.

For example, comfortable walking shoes. Take a pair to work, or even better wear these shoes more often, if possible. Then you'll be ready to go when an opportunity presents itself. Or, if you decide you'd like to drink less coffee and more green tea ensure you have the supplies on hand.

List any supplies you need to get started with **Take 5.**

- Feel like there's NO TIME!? Start taking small breaks and notice how much better you feel. You'll soon be hooked!

Keep your train on the track.

- Use reminders such as reminder bands, stickers or post it notes to remind you to **Take 5.**

- Look for, or create windows of opportunity in your day for Take 5.

- *Keep track to stay on track!!* You can use the Activity Planners provided here to keep track of how you are doing.

- Sign up for the WorkLife Café "Cup of Inspiration" Monthly Newsletter.

- **Get a Take 5 Buddy** ☺

My ideas for keeping the train on the track?

Don't worry if you fall off the track or didn't do as well as planned, just get back on track as soon as possible.

Sometimes journaling or talking with a friend about making changes can help. And remember, often it takes a few attempts to make a successful change. Each time you try you are closer to success. Reminder to always seek professional help when necessary.

Congratulations! You've already taken steps towards a positive change.

I intend to Take 5 towards a healthier, more balanced life, and track my results.

Some of my Take 5 ideas are:

I will reward myself by: _____

Date:_____ **Signed:** _____

CHECK WITH YOUR
DOCTOR BEFORE
STARTING ANY
EXERCISE OR ACTIVITY
PROGRAM

TAKE 5 FORTUNE TELLER

SUSTAIN YOURSELF

TAKE FIVE

4

Call a friend

1

Draw a mind map

5

Take 10 deep breaths

6

Stare into space

8

Stretch

7

Sing a song

3

Drink some water

2

Go for a walk

FEEL ALIVE

TIME FOR YOU

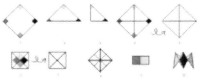

© Copyright. 2010. WorkLife® | WorkLife Balance: for all who struggle to juggle

WORKLIFE CAFE | WEEKLY ACTIVITY PLANNER

Week of _____ **Year** _____

	MONDAY	TUESDAY	WEDNESDAY	THURSDAY	FRIDAY	SATURDAY	SUNDAY
MORNING	ACTIVITY *Go for a walk* ✓	ACTIVITY ○	ACTIVITY ○	ACTIVITY ○	ACTIVITY ○	ACTIVITY ○	ACTIVITY ○
AFTERNOON	ACTIVITY ○	ACTIVITY ○	ACTIVITY ○	ACTIVITY ○	ACTIVITY ○	ACTIVITY ○	ACTIVITY ○
EVENING	ACTIVITY ○	ACTIVITY ○	ACTIVITY ○	ACTIVITY ○	ACTIVITY ○	ACTIVITY ○	ACTIVITY ○

BREATHE DRINK SOME 2 EXERCISE GO 4 A WALK MEDITATE PARTICIPATE TAKE 5

worklifecafe.ca

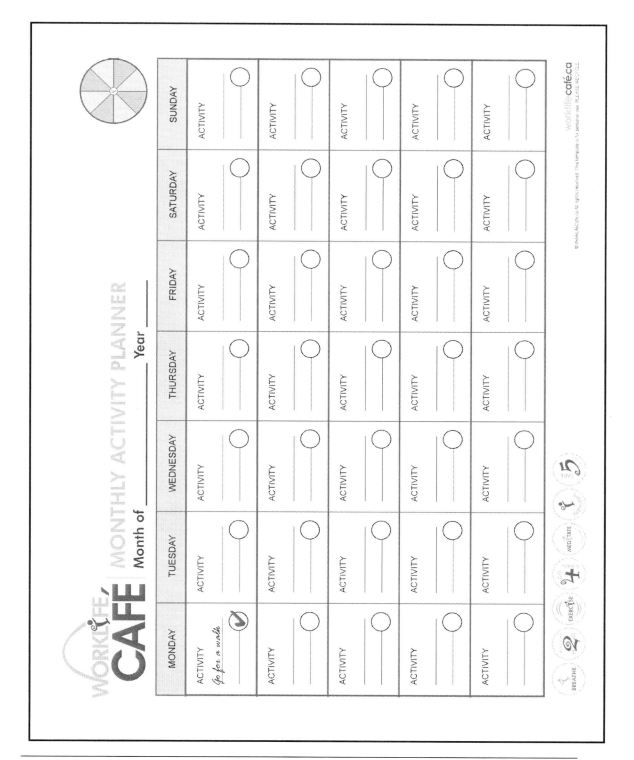

YAY ! I did it. *Over the past month I...*

Make up a **Certificate of Achievement** for yourself and award yourself one of the medals below. ☺

PARTICIPATE MEDALS

WORKLIFECAFÉ

PARTICIPATE

PARTICIPATE

PARTICIPATE

Cut out the individual medals
and pin or tape them to your shirt...
or poke a hole at the top centre.

PLEASE RECYCLE

What did you notice?

Is there anything you would like to do differently?

What will you do more of? What will you do less of?

Keep chugging along...

CHAPTER 6:
GO! FORWARD

Sometimes it seems like we're stuck and it's hard to move forward. Included in this chapter are a few ideas for moving forward: morning writing; plan a day that makes a difference; pick one thing that makes a difference, and Take the Train! Hopefully, you will find something here that may help to nudge you forward. If you want to 'go forward'.

Proceed with Caution! When you work on a creative breakthrough it can create a surge of energy, mean *bumpy ride ahead*, and take you to places you never dreamed possible. Most likely in the direction of your dreams.

Brainstorming Session
M NDMAP

Name

Date

Remember to post in a visible spot!

PLEASE RECYCLE

References & Resources

• Mind Mapping idea from Tony Buzan
• Check out this link for more mind map inspiration
  www.mindmapinspiration.com

THE POWER AND PROMISE OF MORNING WRITING

The solitude of morning is full of power and promise. In early morning it feels like we have the whole world to ourselves. It's the perfect time for bonding with nature through a walk, a run, or a paddle on our favourite lake. It's the perfect time for meditation, quiet reflection, a morning cup of tea, and it's a great time for writing. We wake up full of optimism and ideas, and we can capture this in writing. Throughout history, morning has been recognized as a creative time for artists. Morning writing is worth a try, if you're looking for a creative breakthrough.

I was introduced to the idea of writing morning pages many years ago when I read *The Artist's Way* by Julia Cameron. She has written a trilogy of best-selling books that coach readers to use morning pages. In her first book, morning pages are a component on the *"Spiritual Path to Higher Creativity"* and in her third book, she describes their role in *"The Art of Perseverance."* Tom Bird describes another benefit of morning writing in *The Call of the Writer's Craft: Writing and Selling the Book Within.* Bird insists morning is the *only* productive time for writing *"the book we all have inside of us."*

Here's a few things I've learned from reading and thinking about morning writing.

- Morning can be an extremely effective time for completing writing or other creative work. In the morning we are at our creative best, and the work gets done before the day starts wearing away at us. If you're intimidated by a blank piece of paper, use my Mind Map.

- Writing in the morning can help calm and clear your mind, flush out ideas and solve problems. To focus, try writing the topic at the top of the page. If un-related ideas surface ~ they will ~ Tom Bird suggests leaving a margin on your pages for capturing these thoughts.

- If you're working on a big idea you might want a big un-lined notebook!

- **Proceed with caution!** For me, the experience of morning writing differs considerably depending on the purpose. Writing "morning pages" in the way described, and I believe intended, by Julia Cameron I find calming. Writing in the morning with the intent to meet a deadline often sets my brain racing with ideas for the whole day and even into the night! I keep a notepad on my nightstand for capturing ideas so they don't keep me awake.

Suggested reading:
- Julia Cameron. 1992. *The Artist's Way: A Spiritual Path to Higher Creativity* & 2006. *Finding Water: The Art of Perseverance.*
- Tom Bird. 2009. *Call of the Writer's Craft: Writing and Selling the Book Within.*
- David Lynch. 2006. *Catching the Big Fish: Meditation, Consciousness and Creativity.*

MORNING WRITING

PLAN A "DO DAY" THAT MAKES A DIFFERENCE

Sometimes it seems day after day goes by, filled with routine activities, one day blurring into the next. A day that makes a difference is a day where you dedicate your time and focus to an activity that makes a positive difference in your work-life.

Step 1: Think about a focus for this day and describe it here.

For example: tidy my desk!; research ideas and develop a plan to resolve a problem; work on a major project; get errands done; organize an event for family or friends; or volunteer your time for a community or neighbourhood event. Maybe your "do day" will just be a day to hang out and do nothing but relax and rejuvenate. If others are to be included, or may be impacted by your plan, it's probably best to include them in planning. *Write your idea here.*

| |
| |

Step 2: Brainstorm what it will take to make this day a success.

Brainstorm and list activities and/or resources required to make this day a success. Remember, to keep your budget, time and energy level in mind. Scale back your plan if necessary.

Step 3: Develop your plan and reserve the date.

Confirm your focus for this day. Then list 1 to 3 activities that are do-able and will have the biggest positive impact on achieving your goal. Reserve the date in your planner.

My focus for this day is:
1.
2.
3.
The date and time I have reserved is:

Step 4: List any additional to do's required to make your day a success.

To do:	By this date:

PICK "ONE THING" THAT MAKES A DIFFERENCE

Here's a challenge for you to pick and do one thing that will make a big difference in improving your day-to-day work-life. The purpose of this exercise is to address a key source of frustration or stress, a time-waster, or an energy zapper.

Step 1: Think about things in your life
that are an irritant or source of frustration.

I was thinking about this and realized a frustration and time-waster for me was the design of my purse. It was too narrow to fit my favourite idea capturing notebook, there wasn't a secure spot for my camera, I was always double-checking to make sure my son's epi-pen was 'in there', I was often losing my keys, rushing around looking for them, blaming my husband for misplacing them, (oops) only to find they were in my bag after all, buried at the bottom!

My purse was a daily source of stress. I put finding a new purse on the top of my "do list."

Another example of *one thing that makes a difference*. Every time I wanted to make a cup of tea I was wasting time rifling through my tea collection. I decided to put a small, attractive dish of assorted tea bags near my kettle. Problem solved. Sweet ☺ !

Step 2: Write down something that is causing you frustration,
brainstorm a solution, and think about the benefits.

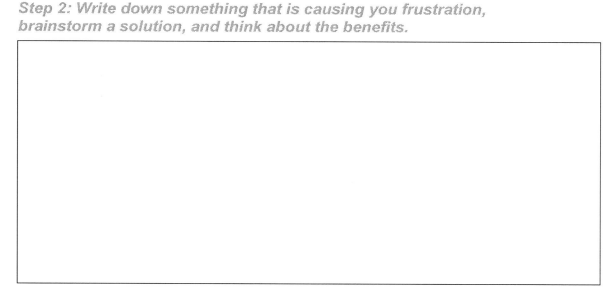

Step 3: Do this now if possible!! or put it on your priority list and schedule
a time.

Step 4: Smile at your cleverness, and repeat as needed.

MAKE A DIFFERENCE

Brainstorming Session
MINDMAP

Name _____

Date _____

Remember to post in a visible spot!

PLEASE RECYCLE

References & Resources
- Mind Mapping idea from Tony Buzan
- Check out this link for more mind map inspiration
  www.mindmapinspiration.com

TAKE THE TRAIN

I came across a little booklet called *"Waiting at the Station"*.[22] This is a story about how people can pass their whole lives waiting on the platform at the train station watching all the trains (opportunities) go by, because they are afraid to get on the train as they are not quite sure of what the journey or the destination will be like.

The metaphor of a train is often used in North American culture. For example, people will say *"I'm off track"* or *"I need to get back on track."* This exercise can be helpful if you feel like you're stuck in a rut or hesitating to pursue a goal. It can help you decide whether to board the train and get on that track. As an added bonus, it's fun!

Make up a "goal" train to remind yourself of your work-life priorities and goals, help you get unstuck, or anytime you want to clarify a goal.

Step 1: Where is your train going? What is a goal you would like to pursue?

Sit quietly and think about a life goal, opportunity or destination as a journey you've considered. Describe that here:

---

[22] 'Take the Train' was inspired by *Waiting at the Station. The (New) Manual for Life*. B. Wong & J. McKeen . (PD Publishing: Gabriola Island, 2001). www.haven.ca.

Step 2: What are your thoughts about the journey?

Do a risk assessment. Consider: *Do you have any thoughts or concerns about taking this journey? Are there any risks? Is there anything holding you back? If yes, what might that be? Would getting on this train be realistic given your current work-life commitments, goals and resources?* If you're worried, think about whether it might be possible to board the train and then get off again if it turns out to be the wrong choice. *Could you board another train? What's the worst thing that could happen?*

Write your thoughts or concerns here.

Note: If this decision could have significant personal, safety, financial or other implications use a more sophisticated analysis !

Step 3: If you decide to take the journey, or even the first leg of the journey, how will your train get there?

Sit quietly and think about the main action/steps required to get "there".

Step 4: Create a goal train and post it in a visible spot.

Write your goal on the train engine and the key next action/steps on the train cars. You can fill out a few of these and put them in your goal book, on a wall, on a dream or vision board, or even in your wallet. Keeping your goals visible is a key to success.

Commit to getting on the train. No more wasting time waiting at the station! Kick it up a notch. Say "Yes" instead of "No" when it doesn't compromise other important goals. Enjoy the journey and keep chugging along.

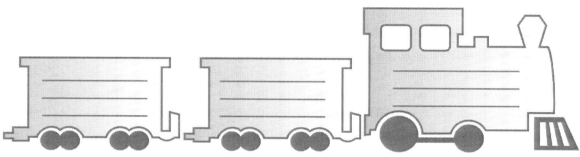

Some other things that are important to me along the journey are:

Step 5: Let your brain, your faith, Mother Earth, the Universe, or the source of guidance on which you rely, guide your train.

Once you've committed to a certain goal or path, and it's on your radar, trust that synchronicity will be on your side and you will be more open to information, opportunities and coincidences that help nudge you along. Often when you fully commit to pursuing something you believe in all the pieces just start falling into place.

CHAPTER 7:
@ WORK

Often the problem behind a lack of work-life balance is **workload**. Workload issues are very difficult to address, particularly in a challenging economy when people are grateful to have a job and reluctant to raise workload concerns.

This chapter includes ideas for giving appreciation and recognition, managing workload, and also a bit of information about Flexible Work Arrangements ~ GET FLEX! Although flexibility may not address workload issues, people often find some relief in their work-life conflict with more flexibility at work. If this is an option with your type of work, and your employer, it might be worth pursuing.

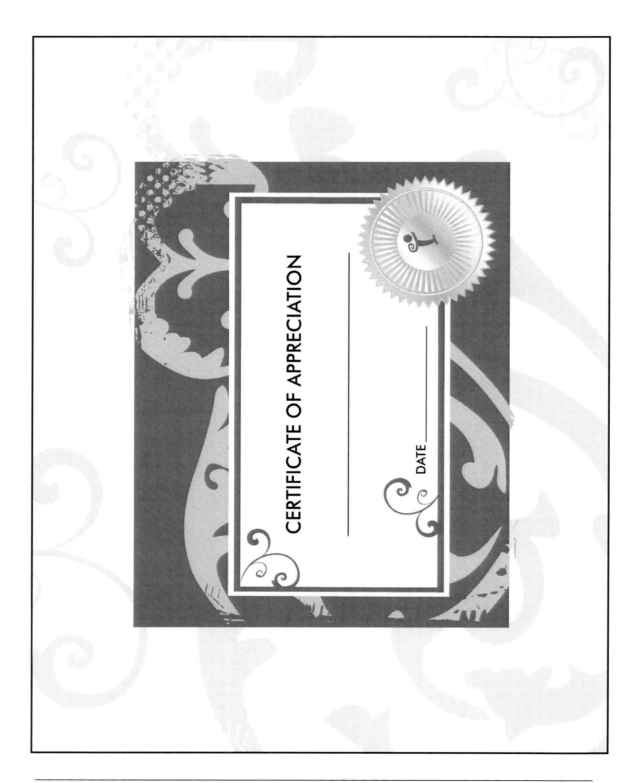

CERTIFICATE OF APPRECIATION

DATE

APPRECIATION AND RECOGNITION

There's not much that we accomplish in life without the support of others. Take 5 and think about people that are close to you and support you. Here's some ideas for showing appreciation and recognition.

Step 1: Make it personal.

When it comes to showing appreciation and giving recognition one-size-does-not-fit-all. There's a growing body of research to support this. So, if you want to give recognition that is meaningful, unless you really know the person and, even if you do, it might be best to ask what they like. If you're a supervisor or manager a great time to do this is during performance planning.

Step 2: Make it timely and specific.

When possible give recognition as soon as possible for a job well done or a special effort. Mention specifically what you noticed and appreciate.

Step 3: Really mean it.

There's not much sense giving appreciation or recognition if the recipient does not feel like it's sincere. People need to know and sense that you really value their contribution. Following the steps above should help to get it right.

Step 4: Now, try it!

Here's an example of how this might look from Terry Small's Brain Bulletin #60 which suggests simple, small celebrations work wonders on your brain and can result in long term change:

> "Hey you did a great job on that assignment!" Or,

> "You put a lot of effort into this. How would you like to celebrate?"

Keep in mind, often what people appreciate most is sincere praise for a job well done.

Want More?

- A beautiful WorkLIfe Café Certificate of Appreciation like the one here is available for download at the WorkLife Café : www.worklifecafe.ca
- Check Terry Small's Website and Brain Bulletins for interesting information about your brain. Did you know current research findings suggest that giving children specific, well-earned praise first thing in the morning or last thing at night has even more of a positive impact http://www.terrysmall.com/index.htm

APPRECIATION AND RECOGNITION

MANAGING WORKLOAD

A key cause of work-life conflict, stress and lack of employee engagement is often Workload. This frequent organizational problem is made worse during challenging economic times when organizations are doing more with less. Here's some ideas that might help with workload.

Step 1: Identify your top 3-5 key responsibilities at work.

Take 5 and find a quiet spot, and identify your top 3 –5 ongoing priorities at work. If you work in a well-managed organization and have a good job description you should already know this. If not ask: *What are the key things that I am responsible for? Which of these activities are most directly related to making the business or organization successful?* This might take some thinking. Often we are distracted at work by activities such as constant emailing. If you write email down, ask yourself whether that activity is really related to your key responsibilities. If the answer is no then better managing your email might be a clue to better managing your workload.

You can also use the WorkLife Framework exercise in Chapter 2 to help confirm and prioritize work goals and assignments.

Step 2: Use your list of key responsibilities to manage workload as follows:

List your key responsibilities and put them on a sticky note in plain view.
Use this sticky note as a constant reminder to help you set your priorities at work. You might want to add Take 5 for healthy breaks to that list of responsibilities. ☺ It might also be a good idea to confirm priorities with your supervisor to make sure you're on the same page. Use your judgement.

Plan your work activities and your day according to your top priorities.
If you are responsible for planning your work ensure you make up your daily, weekly and monthly plan with your key responsibilities in mind. In any job, start the day by asking: *if I could only get 1 thing done today what would be the most important?* Make a plan so you can do that first.

Develop and ask key questions to focus you on your work.
For example; when given the choice of taking on a project you could ask: *how will taking on this project impact my ability to complete other important work assignments; or, get a promotion (if you decide that's important to you)!*

Step 3: Identify your top time wasters, energy zappers and solutions.

Is checking your email every hour distracting you from other work? Think about how you use your time and make note of your key time wasters such as; checking email too often, looking for lost papers, or interruptions.

Write down your top 3 time wasters here. Then read over the ideas for Make Time Your Friend, in this book, to see if there are some ideas you can use as possible solutions.

Challenges:	Solutions:

Step 4: Make a plan.

Make up a rule that suits your job to help you stay on track.
For example: only check email twice a day. If it's important, let your clients know that this is your new work style or advise them of another way to reach you, if necessary. Otherwise, just get to work on your most important task.

Schedule some time in your daily planner to get organized.
No time? Being organized saves time.

If overwhelmed by workload, see tips on the next page.

- **Workload is a serious problem in today's economic climate.** TOO MUCH WORK AND NOT ENOUGH TIME ARE COMMON AND SERIOUS WORKPLACE PROBLEMS THAT CAN LEAVE PEOPLE FEELING OVERWHELMED. If you are feeling overwhelmed at work be sure to ask for help. Hopefully you have a supportive workplace where you can discuss workload issues with your supervisor or human resources department, or utilize the services of your employee assistance program. Also, tell your Dr. or ask for help from family and friends.

- **Don't be a perfectionist unless your work demands it.**

- Flexible Work Arrangements can sometimes help people better manage workload. If you have good work performance, or are struggling to maintain your work performance, flexible work arrangements could benefit both you and your employer. A progressive and supportive workplace and supervisor are key to making flexible work arrangements work. See the GET FLEX! section in the @ Work Chapter for information on Flexible Work Arrangements.

- **If you are out of work**, like many are at the time of writing, or looking for more fulfilling work, I highly recommend Richard Bolles, *Job-hunters' Survival Guide: How to Find Hope and Rewarding Work Even When 'There Are No Jobs'*.

GET FLEX!

If you are working and you don't already have a flexible work arrangement: *have you considered whether more flexibility would help you better manage your work and personal life?* Research shows that typically both employees and employers benefit from flexible work arrangements. Here's a brief overview of FLEX!

What is "Flex"?

Flex refers to Flexible Work Arrangements that give people more control over when, where and how their work gets done. More flexibility at work helps both organizations and individuals deal with challenges resulting from:

- struggling to juggle multiple work-life commitments, including both child and elder-care responsibilities;

- absenteeism and stress-related illness largely attributed to work-life conflict;

- technology contributing to 24/7/365 availability, workload and blurring of lines between work and personal life; and,

- transition to retirement.

In my view, when it comes to working there are three key questions:

- is the work getting done?

- how is the work getting done?

- how well is the working getting done?

Some people predict a future where *people will work anytime, anywhere*. That may be true for some jobs. It's important to keep in mind that flexible work arrangements are easier to implement in some jobs than others.

Typically, flexible work arrangements include changes in; when and how people work, and where people work.

People achieve flexibility in when and how they work through options such as: flex time, job sharing, part-time, contract, compressed work hours, flex days and tele-work.

People achieve flexibility in where they work through options such as working; from home or a remote office, while travelling, or even while caring for sick family members. Changing where you work can be complicated, and even impossible. However, in the majority of cases, given a sincere effort on the part of both employee and employer, flexible work arrangements are possible to implement and generally mutually beneficial.

Who wants FLEX?

These days it seems pretty much everyone wants FLEX! Workplace flexibility and work-life balance are among the top considerations for people of all ages when looking for work. As a bonus, technology has made it easier for some people to work from anywhere, anytime and minimize time loss and the stress and expense of their morning commute.

Research on Work Life Balance shows
- 50% of employees said better work-life balance would make them professionally and personally happier
- 35% of people would rather work shorter hours than win the lottery
- 78% of people interviewed want a better work-life balance. Of these people, 30.5% think their career would suffer if they did. Yet 89% think they would produce stronger results at work if they had a better work-life balance. From Hays, Australia (2010)

The best part is that more and more employers want FLEX! Progressive employers are embracing flexible work arrangements because there is now a mountain of data to show that flexible work arrangements benefit both the employer and employees.

What are the benefits of FLEX?

There is a growing body of research reporting many benefits of flexible work arrangements.

Benefits for people include:

- the ability to more effectively manage the day to day work-life juggle;
- reduced stress and improved health and wellbeing; and,
- the ability to maintain healthy relationships and social connections.

Benefits for workplaces include:

- increased ability to attract and retain a diverse group of talented individuals;
- increased job satisfaction and engagement levels;
- enhanced productivity and profitability; and
- reduced absenteeism.

Benefits for the planet could result from:

- decreased carbon emissions achieved through tele-commuting and other flexible work options that change commuting patterns and reduce power consumption during peak periods.

While there are many benefits associated with flexible work arrangements, there can also be a downside. So, until workplace flexibility policy and practices become more widely adopted it's a good idea to proceed with caution.

Know that requesting and working flexible work arrangements may come with Challenges and Risks.

Here's a few things to keep in mind.

- Remember ~ it's not all about you! When requesting a flexible work arrangement, the priority is to think about how getting your needs met will also meet employer needs and develop your proposal with that in mind.

- Typically flexible work arrangements are viewed as a privilege rather than entitlement.

- Results-based performance is key to success with flexible work arrangements. Demonstrate how you will be able to meet or exceed work expectations.

- Some people working flexible work arrangements believe that they lose out on promotional opportunities because of perceptions like "out of site, out of mind", or beliefs such as "family comes first, work comes second".

- If flexible work arrangements result in a reduction in hours, for instance with part-time or job-sharing, know that benefits, such as leave, pension, employment insurance, etc. will be reduced accordingly.

- You may not want to risk your job by asking for Flex! in a challenging economy. Think about whether the employer could benefit from your request.

- You may feel left out ~ no longer part of the team. Or you may be judged by employees who are not able to FLEX!

- The ultimate form of flexible work arrangements is being self-employed on a full contractual basis. While this may be great for flexibility it usually comes at the expense of benefits such as medical leave, paid vacation, entitlement to employment insurance benefits, pension plans, and means you often end up working all hours of the day and night! Issues related to ensuring people who work on this basis also have some kind of flex-security need to be addressed to successfully move forward with FLEX!

A few interesting things to know about workplace stress and flexibility.

Included earlier, the following two quotes from a feature article in the *Globe and Mail* are worth repeating here. From 'Stress: How Your Busy Life is Killing You.' The front-page lead in reads: *"Work-life balance isn't just a personal challenge – it's a looming public health crisis."*[23]

"The physical and psychological ailments ~ from Alzheimer's and depression to obesity, diabetes and heart disease ~ brought about by stress are believed to be a major reason absentee rates for full-time employees have shot up 21 per cent in the past 10 years. At least 1 think tank estimates that stress-related absences cost employers more than $10 –billion a year, with an additional $14-billion impact on the health-care system."

Harvard researcher Lisa Berman recently studied the impact different types of supervisors can have: *"The stunning thing we found was that managers who scored very low on creativity in managing work-family conflicts had employees who scored much higher in terms of their cardiovascular risk…."*

When it comes to the role of supervisors and work-family conflict, the essentials, it seems, are a supportive manager and supportive workplace culture that allow for some flexibility in work arrangements so that people have, or at least 'perceive' they have more ability to manage the work-life juggle.

I believe what we need most at work is a little wiggle-room and some respect. A little room to take a healthy break, a little room to attend to a family or personal commitment or emergency, and a little respect for our basic need to succeed in both work and life.

At **WorkLife**® we believe in: **Flexibility. Respect. Results.** We promote FLEX! as an opportunity to inspire positive change in the workplace and beyond. We believe in changing the way people work and live, *when the traditional way no longer makes sense.* And we hope you do too![24]

Just Imagine.

Using the Mind Map provided imagine if you had a flexible work arrangement that gave you a little more **wiggle-room.**

What would the ideal arrangement look like? How would flexible work arrangements affect your work-life balance? Consider the BENEFITS, CHALLENGES and any RISKS.

KEY QUESTION: *Can you think of any risks to your job if you request FLEX?*

---

[23] October 30, 2010, (pg: 1, A12-A13)

[24] Our **Get Flex!** *e-book* available @ the WorkLife Café, February 2011.

Brainstorming Session
MINDMAP

Name _____

Date _____

Remember to post in a visible spot!

PLEASE RECYCLE

References & Resources
- Mind Mapping idea from Tony Buzan
- Check out this link for more mind map inspiration
  www.mindmapinspiration.com

worklifecafé.ca
© Copyright 2010 WorkLife. All rights reserved.

- **Great News! A FREE ONE-YEAR MEMBERSHIP TO THE WORKLIFE CAFÉ** is included with your purchase and entitles you to download colourful Workbook Resources. Visit the WorkLife Café at http://www.worklifecafe.ca . Follow the link for Workbook Resources. Type in the username: worklifecafe   password: take5 ~ all lower case.

CHAPTER 8:
ORGANIZE

This chapter includes copies of some of the items in the workbook as well as other popular organizers and planners. These organizers are available through the WorkLife Café website. See the information on the previous page for your **FREE one-year membership** to the WorkLife Café.

BALANCE CHECK ~ (UN) BALANCING FORCES

This is an extra copy of the balance check worksheet in Chapter 1, which is designed to help you to reflect about some of the factors, or in this case forces, that are pushing you out of balance, or pulling you back into balance. Download additional copies at www.worklifecafe.ca

Step 1: Check all that apply, then think about it.

Unbalancing or Pushing Force		Balancing or Pull Force
O In a rut or depressed[25]		O A sense of purpose
O Not enough sleep		O Enough sleep
O Not enough exercise		O Enough exercise
O Too much or NO work		O Work in control
O Worried about money		O Financially secure
O Errands undone		O Errands done
O Family worries		O Family doing well
O Aging Parents	**BALANCE** ▲	O Aging Parents Plan
O No time for friends		O Time with friends
O Unhealthy eating		O Healthy eating
O Not enough Fun ☹		O Enough fun ☺
O Noisy life		O Quiet moments
O Being Late		O Being on time
O Missing Deadlines		O Meeting deadlines
O No real support network		O Support network
What do you need for yourself?		

---

[25] It's critical to seek professional help when overwhelmed or depressed!

BALANCE CHECK ~ (UN) BALANCING FORCES

This is an extra copy of the balance check worksheet in Chapter 1, which is designed to help you to reflect about some of the factors, or in this case forces, that are pushing you out of balance, or pulling you back into balance. Download additional copies at www.worklifecafe.ca

Step 1: Check all that apply, then think about it.

Unbalancing or Pushing Force		Balancing or Pull Force
O In a rut or depressed[26]		O A sense of purpose
O Not enough sleep		O Enough sleep
O Not enough exercise		O Enough exercise
O Too much or NO work		O Work in control
O Worried about money		O Financially secure
O Errands undone		O Errands done
O Family worries	BALANCE	O Family doing well
O Aging Parents		O Aging Parents Plan
O No time for friends		O Time with friends
O Unhealthy eating		O Healthy eating
O Not enough Fun ☹		O Enough fun ☺
O Noisy life		O Quiet moments
O Being Late		O Being on time
O Missing Deadlines		O Meeting deadlines
O No real support network		O Support network
What do you need for yourself?		

---

[26] It's critical to seek professional help when overwhelmed or depressed!

MEMORY KEEPERS: SPECIAL EVENTS

Taking a few minutes now can save you hours in the future trying to re-create history. Even dedicated scrap bookers can benefit from a simple system to capture timely information.

Step 1: Copy or print the WorkLife Cafe Memory Keeper.

- Copy or print the Memory Keeper on acid free paper and complete the key sections, including a photo and other memorabilia.

Step 2: Make a file for your Memory Keeper and other memorabilia.

- If you already have a system in place for preserving memorabilia, congratulations! Use that. If not, use a basic (preferably acid free) file folder. Write the event name and year on the file. Here's some of the items you might want to gather up and save.

    - **Memory Keeper**
    - **Invitations, Ticket Stubs**
    - **Guest lists**
    - **Photos**

Tips:

- *What to keep and what not to keep?* Put hard-to-decide items in a separate file or box and label with event name, year and write "For decision".

- *Items too bulky or large? Can you copy or scan? Can they be framed?* For masterpieces use archival framing which is expensive! if not a department store frame might do. *What about a photo?*

Step 3: File your Memory Keeper and other memorabilia.

- File away your completed Memory Keeper in your alphabetical filing system, special spot for memorabilia or, scan items to your computer for digital scrapbooks.

- If you plan on scrapbooking items make it a date by writing it in your calendar.

Step 4: Reward Yourself for this effort!

MEMORY KEEPER

Date _____

Day _____

Time _____

Special Event _____

Place _____

PHOTO

SPECIAL GIFTS

WHO ATTENDED...

FAVOURITE MEMORY!

worklifecafé.ca
© Copyright 2010 WorkLife. All rights reserved

Inspired by the "Now and Then Child Scrapbook" — Blue Heron Books

MEMORY KEEPERS: SCHOOL YEAR END

School years slip by so quickly and so much memorabilia comes home during these years. Having a system in place for capturing memories can save you hours in the future.

Step 1: Copy or print the WorkLife Cafe Memory Keeper.

Copy or print the Memory Keeper on acid free paper and sit with your child to reflect on their school year and fill in the Memory Keeper blanks. Have some fun!

Step 2: Make a file for your Memory Keeper and other memorabilia.

If you already have a system in place for preserving memorabilia, congratulations! Use that. If not, use a basic (preferably acid free) file folder. Write your child's name and year on the file. Here's some of the items you might want to gather up and save from the mountains of items that find their way home some years:

- **Memory Keeper**
- **Report Card**
- **Best creations ~ art, writing, card …**
- **School photo (s)**
- **A few other key photos or memorabilia**

Tips:

- ***What to keep and what not to keep?*** Put hard-to-decide items in a separate file or box and label with your child's name, year and write "For decision".

- ***Items too bulky or large?*** *Can you copy or scan? Can they be framed?* For *masterpieces* use archival framing which is expensive! if not a department store frame might do. What about a photo? You can lay out favourite pieces on the floor and photograph. Or, *maybe* your child will pose with their favourite artwork.

- **This is a good time to think about whether you have a good photo of your child from the year.** You can take photos now!

Step 3: File your Memory Keeper and other memorabilia.

- File away your completed Memory Keeper in your alphabetical filing system, special spot for school memorabilia or, scan items to your computer for digital scrapbooks.

Step 4: Reward Yourself!

MEMORY KEEPER

Name _____

Grade _____

Year _____

Teacher _____

School _____

MY PHOTO

MY SIGNATURE

FAVOURITE...

Colour _____

Book _____

Movie _____

Food _____

Place _____

Song _____

Game _____

Sport _____

FAVOURITE MEMORIES!

worklifecafé.ca
© Copyright 2010 WorkLife. All rights reserved.

Inspired by the "Now and Then Child Scrapbook" — Blue Heron Books.

- **Remember, life is better with balance.** I'm reminded of a skit about scrapbooking on CBC Television's, *This Hour has 22 Minutes*. The comedian brought out a cart of scrapbooking supplies and mocked the time-consuming art of scrapbooking, concluding the skit with the line: *"After all, why live life when you can scrapbook it?"*

CHAPTER 9:
JUST FOR FUN

Sometimes all we need to relieve stress and take a healthy work-life break is a little fun. Make it easy to include more fun and games in your day-to-day routine! Keep a chess set or a game that's quick to play handy, or use one of the Fortune Tellers in this chapter to make things fun.

And here's the fun part! Beautiful colour copies of the worksheets, planners and fun stuff in this Workbook are available to download for **FREE, for one year**, with your purchase of this book. Visit the WorkLife Café at http://www.worklifecafe.ca . Follow the link for Free Resources. Type in the username: worklifecafe   password: take5 ~ all lower case.

TOP 10
Ways to tell if you have Cabin Fever...

- ○ You start calling telemarketers
- ○ Everything you say is funny
- ○ Everything you say is NOT funny
- ○ Manners, what manners?
- ○ Your pj's start looking like a 3-piece suit
- ○ The dog hides on you
- ○ Every day is a bad hair day
- ○ Nonsense starts to make sense
- ○ Get up, why?
- ○ The birds are scared to come to your bird feeder

IT'S DEFINITELY TIME TO GETAWAY!!

PLEASE RECYCLE

WORKLIFE FUN:

Fortune Teller: How to Make and Play

How to Make:
- Cut on the dotted line border of the Fortune Teller.
- Fold diagonally into a triangle, then unfold and repeat in the opposite way to make a centre point.
- Turn the Fortune Teller over, right side down.
- Fold each corner to meet at the centre point, on top.
- Turn the paper over again, I guy facing you, numbers down.
- Again, fold each corner to meet at the centre point. Now you have a small square with numbers facing up.
- With the numbers facing you, fold the Fortune Teller in half, so that the number sides are touching.
- While still folded in half put your thumb and first finger of each hand into the 4 flaps. This is a bit tricky.
- Keep your fingers underneath and press the corners together til it moves smoothly.

How to Play:
- First chose a topic then open the Fortune Teller to show the numbers.
- Then, choose a number and open and close the fortune teller that many times.
- Lastly, pick a number again, open that flap and read what's written.

- On Your own: Take 5 ~ the fortune teller can help you choose an activity to sustain yourself or just for fun!
- At work: Take 5 with your co-workers to pick up the energy level, spark creativity, take a quick break or just for fun!
- At play: Take 5 with family and friends to start a conversation or help choose a fun activity.
- Waiting and Traveling: stuck in traffic or a line up with the kids or friends ~ pull out a Fortune Teller and pass the time in a fun way.
- For learning something new: Take 5 to learn about something new in a fun way.

Tips:
- Fortune Tellers can be printed on the back of a used piece of paper, and recycled when you've done having fun or saved for another time. Please recycle.
- Respect that some people may not want to play fortune teller : (maybe they don't think it's fun or they are just too busy.
- Find more Fortune Tellers at the WorkLife Café: http://www.workLifecafe.ca.

PLEASE RECYCLE

WORKLIFECAFÉ

HOUSECLEANING FORTUNE TELLER

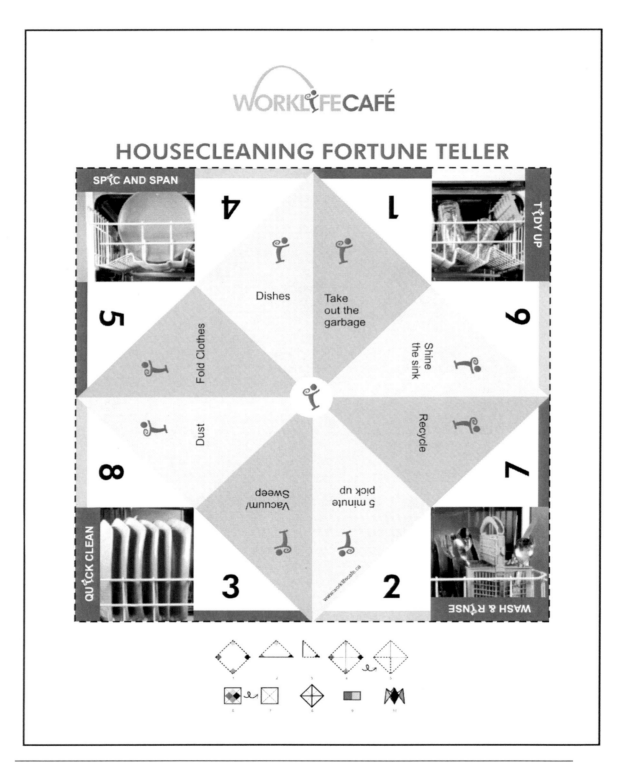

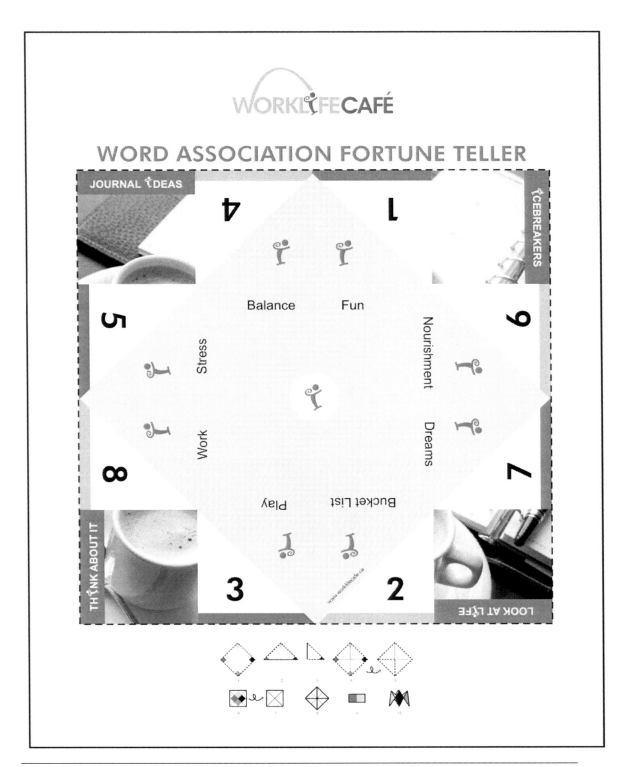

WORD ASSOCIATION FORTUNE TELLER

JOURNAL IDEAS

ICEBREAKERS

4

1

Balance   Fun

5

6

Stress

Nourishment

Work

Dreams

8

7

Play   Bucket List

www.worklifecafe.ca

3

2

THINK ABOUT IT

LOOK AT LIFE

OFFICE CLEAN FORTUNE TELLER

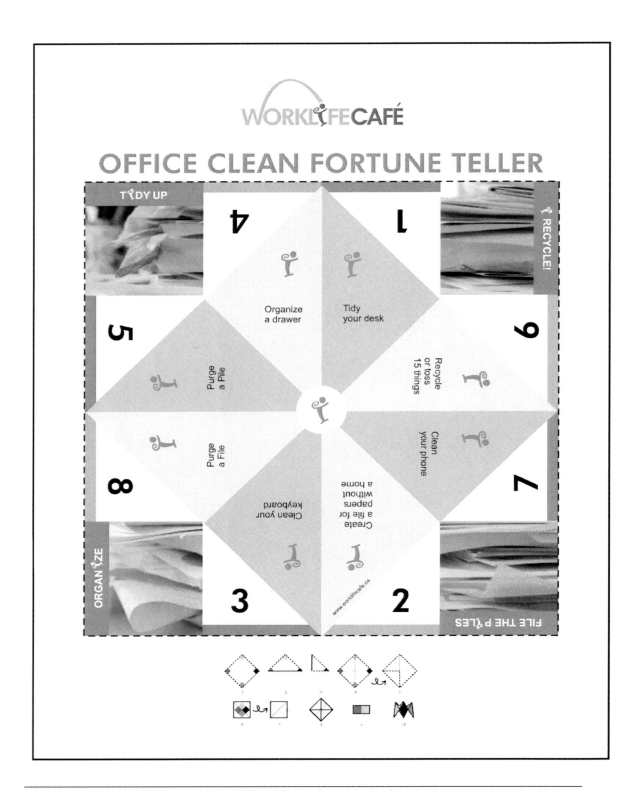

Sometimes[27]

Sometimes you know
Sometimes you don't know
    When...it's the last time you will:
        See him
        See her
        Eat that food
        Sit in that chair
        Smell a smell
        Hear her laugh
            Feel his skin
            Touch her
            Kiss her
        Shake his hand
        Walk that peaceful trail
        Eat at your favourite restaurant
        Drive there
        Pet your dog
        Cuddle your cat
            Ride your horse
            Kick that ball
            Eat bacon
See the dimple on your child's hand
Sleep with your baby
Hear your son's voice, before it changes

---

[27] By Michael D. Blackstock, with permission. (Oceaness, 2010)

References

Ideas and inspiration included in this book have come from the following authors and books.

Bachelard, Gaston. 1942. *Water and Dreams.* The Dallas Institute of Humanities and Culture. Texas.

Bennko, Cathleen & Weisberg, Anne. 2007. *Mass Career Customization. Aligning the Workplace with Today's Non-Traditional Workforce.* Harvard Business School Press. Waterton. MA.

Biddulph, Steve. 2004. *The Secrets of Happy Parents: how to stay in love as a couple and true to yourself. Thorsons: Wellingborough.*

Bolles, Richard Nelson. *What Colour is Your Parachute*, updated annually, and *Parachute WorkBook*. Ten Speed Press. Berkeley.

Bricker, Darrell & Wright, John. *What Canadians Think: About Almost Everything.* 2005. Seal Books.

Buck Consultants. 2009. *Global Wellness Survey.*

Buettner, Dan. Nov. 2005. The Secrets of Living Longer. *National Geographic.* National Geographic Society. Washington D.C. http://ngm.nationalgeographic.com/ngm/0511/feature1/index.html

Buzan, Tony. 2006. *Mind Mapping: KickStart Your Creativity and Transform Your Life.* BBC Active. London.

Cameron, Julia. 1992. *The Artist's Way: A Spiritual Path to Higher Creativity* (Inner Workbook). Tarcher. New York.

Cameron, Julia. 2006. *Finding Water: The Art of Perseverance.* Tarcher. New York.

Canfield, Jack. 2007. *The Success Principles: How to get from where you are to where you want to be.* Harper Collins. New York.

Corporate Executive Board. 2009. *The Increasing Call for Work-Life Balance.* http://www.executiveboard.com/businessweek/bw-week9.html

Covey, Stephen. 1990. *The 7 Habits of Highly Effective People.* Free Press. New York.

Csikszentmihalyi, Mihaly. 1997. *Finding Flow: The Psychology of Engagement with Everyday Life.* Basic Books/Persues Books Group. New York.

Doidge, Norman. 2007. *The Brain that Changes Itself.* Penguin. New York.

Duxbury, Linda and Higgins, Chris. 2008. *Reducing Work-Life Conflict; What works? What doesn't?* Health Canada: Ottawa.

Evans, Carol. 2006. *This Is How We Do It: the Working Mothers' Manifesto.* Hudson Street Press.

Gibbs, Nancy. *Time.com, Sunday,* Jun. 04, 2006. 'The Magic of the Family Meal.'

Honore, Carl. 2004. *In Praise of SLOW: How a Worldwide Movement is Challenging the Cult of Speed.* Vintage. Toronto.

Hyman, M. 2009. *The UltraMind Solution. The Simple Way to Defeat Depression, Overcome Anxiety, and Sharpen Your Mind.* Scribner. New York.

Izzo, John and Withers, Pam. 2001. *Values-Shift: The New Work Ethic and what it means for business.* Fairwinds Press. Vancouver.

Jaworski, Joseph. 1996. *Synchronicity: The Inner Path of Leadership.* Berrett-Kohler. San Francisco.

Kelliher, Clare with Anderson, Deirdre. 2008. *Flexible Working and Performance.* Cranfield School of Management, in conjunction with Working Families (UK) http://www.workingfamilies.org.uk/ and corporate sponsors.

McGee-Cooper, Anne. 1992. *You Don't Have to Go Home from Work Exhausted: A Program to Bring Joy, Energy, and Balance to Your Life.* Bantam: New York.

Morgenstern, Julia. 2005. Fireside, Philadelphia. *Never Check Email in the Morning.*

Prochaska, Jo et al. 1994. *Changing for Good. The revolutionary program that explains the sic stages of change and teaches you how to free yourself from bad habits.* Morrow. New York.

Ramsland, Marcia. 2006. *Simplify Your Time: Stop Running and Start Living.* Thomas Nelson. Nashville.

Richardson, Cheryl. 1999. *Take Time for Your Life.* Three Rivers Press. New York.

Schumacher, E.F. 1973. *Small is Beautiful: Economics as if people mattered.*

Senge, Peter. 1994. *The Fifth Discipline: The Art & Practice of The Learning Organization.* Doubleday. New York.

Shecter, Lara. 2004. *"Now and Then"* : The Coolest Scrapbook for school-aged children. Blue Heron Books. Comox. (Memory Keeper Idea)

Welch, Suzy. 2009. *10-10-10: A Life Transforming Idea.* Scribner. New York.

Wong, Ben and McKeen, Jock. 2001. *The (New) Manual for Life.* PD Publishing: Gabriola Island.

Yerkes, Leslie. 2001. *Fun Works: Creating Places Where People Love to Work.* Berrett-Koehler. San Francisco.

Various. Inter-disciplinary team of Researchers. 1960's. **Roseto Effect** and the importance of social networks in health and longevity at http://www.uic.edu/classes/osci/osci590/14_2 The Roseto Effect.htm

Zelinski, Ernie. 1997. *The Joy of Not Working.* Ten Speed Press. Berkeley.

REFERENCES AND RESOURCES

Web Resources ~

David Allen, *Getting Things Done.* http://www.davidco.com/

Canadian Centre for Occupational Health and Safety http://www.ccohs.ca/healthyworkplaces

Canada's *Globe and Mail* Our Time to Lead: Work-Life Balance
http://www.theglobeandmail.com/news/national/time-to-lead/work-life-balance/

Linda Duxbury, Chris Higgins, et al. have been an instrumental in defining the Canadian work-life landscape, in particular work-life conflict, and documenting what works and what doesn't work. Key research reports on work-life balance can be found here: http://www.hc-sc.gc.ca/ewh-semt/pubs/occup-travail/index-eng.php

Fly Lady coaching and organizing http://www.flylady.net/

Maslow's *Hierarchy of Needs* diagram, recreated from one found on www through Google images. Crème-de-languedoc.com

Polestar Calendars http://www.polestarcalendars.com/index.php

Public Health Agency of Canada (Active Living at Work) http://www.phac-aspc.gc.ca/hp-ps/hl-mvs/pa-ap/index-eng.php

Terry Small's Brain Bulletins http://www.terrysmall.com/index.htm

The World Café http://www.theworldcafe.com/

WorkLife® HR Solutions: Flexibility. Respect. Results http://www.worklife.ca

WorkLife Café

- WorkLife Café Website http://www.worklifecafe.ca/
- WorkLife Café Bookstore http://astore.amazon.ca/worcaf-20
- *WorkLife Balance: (WorkBook) for all who struggle to juggle*
- WorkLife Workshops
- WorkLife Monthly Newsletter ~ *a cup of inspiration*

About the Author

Charlene Levis, MA, CHRP is the founder of **WorkLife®** HR Solutions http://www.worklife.ca and the WorkLife Café. Charlene is a Certified Human Resources Professional (CHRP) with 20 years of HR experience, and is an internationally recognized contributor in the work-life field.

Charlene established the WorkLife Café, and wrote *WorkLife Balance: for all who struggle to juggle!* to provide ideas, information and inspiration in a worklife-friendly format to help people to find a happy and healthy synchronicity between work and life. Charlene works flexible hours from her home-based office so that she can manage the work-life juggle.

About the Designer

Sandra Verhoeff has her BA with a major in Art and has been working as a graphic designer for over 20 years. She enjoys creating beautifully-designed marketing materials, complete with logos, stationery, booklets, brochures, bookmarks and any other print material necessary for a successful corporate image and brand. http://www.signetstudio.com